KOREAN

VISUAL DICTIONARY

Published by Collins
An imprint of HarperCollins Publishers
Westerhill Road
Bishopbriggs
Glasgow G64 2QT

HarperCollins*Publishers*
Macken House,
39/40 Mayor Street Upper,
Dublin 1, D01 C9W8, Ireland

First Edition 2021

10 9 8 7 6 5 4 3

© HarperCollins Publishers 2021

ISBN 978-0-00-839963-4

Collins® is a registered trademark of
HarperCollins Publishers Limited

Typeset by Jouve, India

Printed in India

A catalogue record for this book is available
from the British Library

If you would like to comment on any aspect
of this book, please contact us at the given
address or online.
E-mail dictionaries@harpercollins.co.uk
www.facebook.com/collinsdictionary
@collinsdict

MANAGING EDITOR
Maree Airlie

FOR THE PUBLISHER
Gerry Breslin
Kerry Ferguson
Gina Macleod
Kevin Robbins
Robin Scrimgeour

CONTRIBUTORS
Myunghae Seo
Anna Stevenson

TECHNICAL SUPPORT
Claire Dimeo

Acknowledgements

We would like to thank those authors and
publishers who kindly gave permission for
copyright material to be used in the Collins
Corpus. We would also like to thank Times
Newspapers Ltd for providing valuable data.

MIX
Paper | Supporting
responsible forestry
FSC™ C007454

This book is produced from independently certified FSC™
paper to ensure responsible forest management.

For more information visit: **www.harpercollins.co.uk/green**

CONTENTS

4   **INTRODUCTION**

7   **THE ESSENTIALS**

19   **TRANSPORT**

49   **IN THE HOME**

73   **AT THE SHOPS**

117   **DAY-TO-DAY**

147   **LEISURE**

173   **SPORT**

197   **HEALTH**

225   **PLANET EARTH**

247   **CELEBRATIONS AND FESTIVALS**

257   **INDEX**

Whether you're on holiday or staying for a slightly longer period of time, your **Collins Visual Dictionary** is designed to help you find exactly what you need, when you need it. With over a thousand clear and helpful images, you can quickly locate the vocabulary you are looking for.

THE DINING ROOM | 식사공간

The kitchen and dining area are generally combined in Korean homes. People may invite close friends to their homes for a meal, but otherwise they generally prefer to invite people out to a restaurant.

YOU MIGHT SAY/HEAR...

② Thank you for the meal I'm going to have.
잘 먹겠습니다.
jal meokgetseumnida

③ Thank you for the meal I had.
잘 먹었습니다.
jal meogeotseumnida

VOCABULARY

④

dining table	tablecloth	to dine
식탁	식탁보	식사하다
siktak	siktakbo	siksahada
sideboard	to set the table	to clear the table
수납장	밥상을 차리다	밥상을 치우다
sunapjang	bapsangeul charida	bapsangeul chiuda

YOU SHOULD KNOW...

⑤ Good table manners in Korea include: waiting for the most senior person at the table to start; not hitting the spoons or chopsticks on the bowl or standing them upright in the rice; and not standing up to reach a dish.

GENERAL

①

knife and fork	Korean teacup	mug
나이프와 포크	찻잔	머그잔
naipeuwa pokeu	chatjan	meogeujan

63

4

The Visual Dictionary includes:

- 10 chapters arranged thematically, so that you can easily find what you need to suit the situation
- **①** **images** – illustrating essential items
- **②** **YOU MIGHT SAY...** – common phrases that you might want to use
- **③** **YOU MIGHT HEAR...** – common phrases that you might come across
- **④** **VOCABULARY** – common words that you might need
- **⑤** **YOU SHOULD KNOW...** – tips about local customs or etiquette
- an **index** to find all images quickly and easily
- essential **phrases** and **numbers** listed on the flaps for quick reference

USING YOUR COLLINS VISUAL DICTIONARY

The points set out below will help to make sure that your **Collins Visual Dictionary** gives you as much help as possible when using Korean:

1) Word order

Korean word order is subject – object – verb. However, when the topic or subject can be understood among the speakers or from the context, it is often omitted. Personal pronouns are avoided; instead, the person's name or the appropriate way of addressing the person is used.

2) How to address people politely

You should not call family members by name unless they are from a younger generation. More information about terms of address for relatives can be found on pages 10 and 11.

The gender-neutral suffix, 씨 (ssi), is similar to Mr/Miss/Ms in English and can be used as a polite way to address someone who is of a similar age or social position. With junior or younger colleagues at work, you use their name followed by the gender-neutral suffix, for example, 김소영 (Kim Soyeong) would be called 김소영 씨 (Kim Soyeong ssi) or 소영 씨 (Soyeong ssi). With senior or older colleagues, the name and the position of the person would be used followed by the gender-neutral honorific suffix 님 (nim). For example, a manager called 김소영 (Kim Soyeong) would be known as 김소영 부장님 (Kim Soyeong bujangnim) or, giving only the surname, 김 부장님 (Kim bujangnim).

3) Verb forms

There are different levels of politeness in Korean, and polite forms suitable for use among family, friends, and colleagues have been used in the phrases in this book. When the verb ends in a consonant, 이에요 (ieyo) follows; when the verb ends in a vowel, 예요 (yeyo) follows. Adding the honorific form, (으)시 ((eu)si), makes the form more polite.

4) Particles

Korean uses words called particles to show how different parts of the sentence relate to each other. Some work in a similar way to English prepositions, but in Korean they are typically attached to nouns. For example, in the sentence 저는 점심을 먹었어요 (jeoneun jeomsimeul meogeosseoyo) meaning "I had lunch", 저 (jeo) meaning "I" is a topic in this sentence, followed by 는 (neun) as the topic particle, and 점심 (jeomsim) meaning "lunch" is an object, followed by 을 (eul) as the object particle. Note that the topic and object particles are often omitted, so 저 점심 먹었어요 (jeo jeomsim meogeosseoyo) is also correct.

5) Number systems

There are two number systems in Korean, sino Korean and native Korean. Sino Korean numbers (shown on the inside cover of the book) are used to count seconds and minutes, to talk about the date and money, and to give phone numbers. The native Korean number system shown below is used to count hours, and to talk about age and numbers of people or things.

Number	Native Korean		Number	Native Korean	
1	하나/한	(hana/han)	15	열다섯	(yeoldaseot)
2	둘/두	(dul/du)	16	열여섯	(yeoryeoseot)
3	셋/세	(set/se)	17	열일곱	(yeorilgop)
4	넷/네	(net/ne)	18	열여덟	(yeoryeodeol)
5	다섯	(daseot)	19	열아홉	(yeorahop)
6	여섯	(yeoseot)	20	스물	(seumul)
7	일곱	(ilgop)	30	서른	(seoreun)
8	여덟	(yeodeol)	40	마흔	(maheun)
9	아홉	(ahop)	50	쉰	(swin)
10	열	(yeol)	60	예순	(yesun)
11	열하나	(yeolhana)	70	일흔	(ilheun)
12	열둘	(yeoldul)	80	여든	(yeodeun)
13	열셋	(yeolset)	90	아흔	(aheun)
14	열넷	(yeollet)	100	No native Korean after 99	

FREE AUDIO

We have created a free audio resource to help you learn and practise the Korean words for all of the images shown in this dictionary. The Korean words in each chapter are spoken by native speakers, giving you the opportunity to listen to each word twice and repeat it yourself. Download the audio from the website below to learn all of the vocabulary you need for communicating in Korean.

www.collins.co.uk/visualdictionary

Whether you're going to be visiting Korea, or even staying there for a while, you'll want to be able to chat with people and get to know them better. Being able to communicate effectively with acquaintances, friends, family, and colleagues is key to becoming more confident in Korean in a variety of everyday situations.

umbrella
우산
usan

blue
파란색
paransaek

red
빨간색
ppalgansaek

green
초록색
choroksaek

yellow
노란색
noransaek

white
하얀색
hayansaek

black
검은색
geomeunsaek

THE BASICS | 기본 어휘 및 표현

Hello!/Hi!
안녕하세요!
annyeonghaseyo

Good night.
안녕히 주무세요.
annyeonghi jumuseyo

See you tomorrow.
내일 만나요.
naeil mannayo

Good morning.
좋은 아침이에요.
joeun achimieyo

See you soon.
또 만나요.
tto mannayo

Have a good day!
좋은 하루 보내세요!
joeun haru bonaeseyo

YOU SHOULD KNOW...

There are two ways of saying goodbye in Korea. If you are leaving but the person you are talking to is staying, you say 안녕히 계세요 (annyeonghi gyeseyo). However, if you are staying but the person you are talking to is leaving, or you are both are leaving, you say 안녕히 가세요 (annyeonghi gaseyo).

Yes.
네.
ne

Thank you.
감사합니다.
gamsahamnida

I'm sorry.
죄송합니다.
joesonghamnida

No.
아니요.
aniyo

No, thanks.
아니요,
괜찮습니다.
aniyo,
gwaenchansseumnida

OK!
알았어요!
arasseoyo

I don't know.
모르겠어요.
moreugesseoyo

You're welcome.
천만에요.
cheonmaneyo

Excuse me.
실례합니다.
sillyehamnida

please
부탁합니다
butakamnida

Sorry?
네?
ne

I don't understand.
이해가 안 돼요.
ihaega an dwaeyo

Yes, please.
네, 부탁합니다.
ne, butakamnida

8

How old are you?
나이가 어떻게
되세요?

naiga eotteoke doeseyo

When is your birthday?
생일이 언제예요?

saengniri eonjeyeyo

I'm ... years old.
... 살이에요.

... sarieyo

I was born in...
... 에서 태어났어요.

... eseo taeeonasseoyo

Where do you live?
어디 사세요?

eodi saseyo

Where are you from?
어디에서 오셨어요?

eodieseo osyeosseoyo

I'm from...
... 에서 왔어요.

... eseo wasseoyo

I live in...
... 에 살아요.

... e sarayo

I'm...
저는 ...이에요.

jeoneun ...ieyo

British
영국 사람

yeongguk saram

Scottish
스코틀랜드 사람

seukoteullaendeu saram

English
잉글랜드 사람

inggeullaendeu saram

Irish
아일랜드 사람

aillaendeu saram

Welsh
웨일스 사람

weilseu saram

Are you married/single?
결혼했어요/
솔로예요?

gyeolhonhaesseoyo/
solloyeyo

I'm married.
결혼했어요.

gyeolhonhaesseoyo

I have a partner.
배우자가 있어요.

baeujaga isseoyo

I'm single.
솔로예요.

solloyeyo

I'm divorced.
이혼했어요.

ihonhaesseoyo

I'm widowed.
사별했어요.

sabyeolhaesseoyo

Do you have any
children?
아이가 있어요?

aiga isseoyo

I have ... children.
아이가 ... 있어요.

aiga ... isseoyo

I don't have any
children.
아이가 없어요.

aiga eopseoyo

YOU SHOULD KNOW...

You might be asked about your age, occupation, or even your relationship status by people who are not that close to you. Don't be offended, this is part of the Korean culture, although people's views on privacy are starting to change.

This is my...
여기는 제 ...
이에요/예요.
yeogineun je ... ieyo/yeyo

These are my...
이들은 제 ...
이에요/예요.
ideureun je ... ieyo/yeyo

husband
남편
nampyeon

wife
아내
anae

boyfriend
남자 친구
namja chingu

girlfriend
여자 친구
yeoja chingu

partner
배우자
baeuja

fiancé/fiancée
약혼자/약혼녀
yakonja/yakonnyeo

son
아들
adeul

daughter
딸
ttal

parents
부모님
bumonim

mother
어머니
eomeoni

father
아버지
abeoji

younger brother
남동생
namdongsaeng

younger sister
여동생
yeodongsaeng

older brother
형/오빠
hyeong/oppa

older sister
누나/언니
nuna/eonni

grandfather
할아버지
harabeoji

grandmother
할머니
halmeoni

granddaughter
손녀
sonnyeo

grandson
손자
sonja

mother-in-law
(*husband's mother*)
시어머니
sieomeoni

YOU SHOULD KNOW...

In Korean, you use a different word for 'older brother' and 'older sister' depending on whether you are male or female. In the examples given above, the first translation is used if you are male, and the second one if you are female.

mother-in-law
(*wife's mother*)
장모님
jangmonim

father-in-law
(*husband's father*)
시아버지
siabeoji

father-in-law
(*wife's father*)
장인어른
jangineoreun

daughter-in-law
며느리
myeoneuri

son-in-law
사위
sawi

stepmother
새어머니
saeeomeoni

stepfather
새아버지
saeabeoji

stepson
의붓아들
uibusadeul

stepdaughter
의붓딸
uibutttal

nephew
조카
joka

niece
조카딸
jokattal

cousin
사촌
sachon

extended family
대가족
daegajok

friend
친구
chingu

baby
아기
agi

child
아이
ai

teenager
십대
sipdae

YOU SHOULD KNOW...

The Korean words you use for 'brother-in-law' and 'sister-in-law' vary, depending on whether you are male or female, how old you are in relation to your in-laws, and what your relationship is. Similarly, 'uncle' and 'aunt' have different translations in Korean according to their marital status and relationship to you.

How are you?
잘 지내세요?
jal jinaeseyo

How's it going?
어떻게 지내요?
eotteoke jinaeyo

Very well, thanks, and you?
저는 잘 지내요.
고마워요. 어떻게 지내요?
jeoneun jal jinaeyo.
gomawoyo. eotteoke jinaeyo

Great!
대단해요!
daedanhaeyo

So-so.
그저 그래요.
geujeo geuraeyo

I'm fine.
잘 지내요.
jal jinaeyo

I'm tired.
피곤해요.
pigonhaeyo

I'm hungry/thirsty.
배 고파요/목 말라요.
bae gopayo/mok mallayo

I'm cold.
추워요.
chuwoyo

I'm warm.
더워요.
deowoyo

I feel... / I am...
저는...
jeoneun...

happy
행복해요
haengbokaeyo

excited
신나요
sinnayo

surprised
놀랐어요
nollasseoyo

annoyed
짜증나요
jjajeungnayo

sad
슬퍼요
seulpeoyo

worried
걱정돼요
geokjeongdwaeyo

afraid
무서워요
museowoyo

bored
지루해요
jiruhaeyo

well
건강해요
geonganghaeyo

unwell
몸이 아파요
momi apayo

better
좋아졌어요
joajyeosseoyo

worse
더 안 좋아요
deo an joayo

Where do you work?
어디에서 일
하세요?
eodieseo il haseyo

What do you do?
어떤 일 하세요?
eotteon il haseyo

What's your occupation?
직업이 뭐예요?
jigeobi mwoyeyo

Do you work/study?
일해요/공부해요?
ilhaeyo/gongbuhaeyo

I'm self-employed.
자영업을 해요.
jayeongeobeul haeyo

I'm unemployed.
무직이에요.
mujigieyo

I'm at university.
대학교에 다녀요.
daehakgyoe danyeoyo

I'm retired.
은퇴했어요.
euntoehaesseoyo

I'm travelling.
여행 다녀요.
yeohaeng danyeoyo

I work from home.
집에서 일해요
jibeseo ilhaeyo

I work part-/full-time.
시간제로/
전일제로 일해요.
siganjero/jeoniljero ilhaeyo

I'm a/an...
저는 ... 이에요/
예요.
jeoneun ... ieyo/yeyo

builder
건설 노동자
geonseol nodongja

chef
주방장
jubangjang

civil servant
공무원
gongmuwon

cleaner
청소부
cheongsobu

dentist
치과 의사
chigwa uisa

doctor
의사
uisa

driver
기사
gisa

electrician
전기기술자
jeongigisulja

engineer
기술자
gisulja

farmer
농부
nongbu

firefighter
소방관
sobanggwan

fisherman
어부
eobu

IT worker
IT 기술자
IT gisulja

joiner
소목장이
somokjangi

journalist
기자
gija

lawyer
변호사
byeonhosa

13

mechanic
정비공
jeongbigong

soldier
군인
gunin

government
정부
jeongbu

nurse
간호사
ganhosa

teacher
선생님
seonsaengnim

hospital
병원
byeongwon

office worker
회사원
hoesawon

vet
수의사
suuisa

hotel
호텔
hotel

plumber
배관공
baegwangong

waiter/waitress
종업원
jongeobwon

office
사무실
samusil

police officer
경찰관
gyeongchalgwan

I work at/in...
... 에서 일해요.
... eseo ilhaeyo.

restaurant
식당
sikdang

sailor
선원
seonwon

business
사업
saeop

school
학교
hakgyo

salesperson
판매원
panmaewon

company
회사
hoesa

shop
가게
gage

scientist
과학자
gwahakja

factory
공장
gongjang

morning
아침
achim

afternoon
점심
jeomsim

evening
저녁
jeonyeok

night
밤
bam

midday
정오
jeongo

midnight
자정
jajeong

What time is it?
몇 시예요?
myeot siyeyo

It's nine o'clock.
아홉시예요.
ahopsiyeyo

It's quarter past nine.
아홉시
십오분이에요.
ahopsi sibobunieyo

It's half past nine.
아홉시 반이에요.
ahopsi banieyo

It's quarter to ten.
열시 십오분
전이에요.
yeolsi sibobun jeonieyo

It's 10 a.m.
오전 열시예요.
ojeon yeolsiyeyo

It's 5 p.m.
오후 다섯시예요.
ohu daseotsiyeyo

It's 17:30.
십칠시
삼십분이에요.
sipchilsi samsipbunieyo

When...?
언제...?
eonje...

... in 60 seconds.
육십초 안에...
yuksipcho ane...

... in two minutes.
이분 안에...
ibun ane...

... in an hour.
한시간 안에...
hansigan ane...

... in quarter of an hour.
십오분 안에...
sibobun ane...

... in half an hour.
삼십분 안에...
samsipbun ane...

early
일찍
iljjik

late
늦게
neutge

soon
곧
got

later
나중에
najunge

now
지금
jigeum

Monday	Wednesday	Friday	Sunday
월요일	수요일	금요일	일요일
woryoil	suyoil	geumyoil	iryoil

Tuesday	Thursday	Saturday	
화요일	목요일	토요일	
hwayoil	mogyoil	toyoil	

January	April	July	October
일월	사월	칠월	시월
irwol	sawol	chirwol	siwol

February	May	August	November
이월	오월	팔월	십일월
iwol	owol	parwol	sibirwol

March	June	September	December
삼월	유월	구월	십이월
samwol	yuwol	guwol	sibiwol

day	month	weekly
일	월	매주
il	wol	maeju

weekend	year	fortnightly
주말	년	격주로
jumal	nyeon	gyeokjuro

week	decade	monthly
주	십년	매달
ju	simnyeon	maedal

fortnight	daily	yearly
보름	매일	매년
boreum	maeil	maenyeon

today
오늘
oneul

tonight
오늘 밤
oneul bam

tomorrow
내일
naeil

yesterday
어제
eoje

the day after tomorrow
모레
more

the day before
yesterday
그저께
geujeokke

on Mondays
월요일에
woryoire

every Sunday
일요일마다
iryoilmada

last Thursday
지난 목요일
jinan mogyoil

next Friday
다음 금요일
daeum geumyoil

the week before
지지난 주
jijinan ju

the week after
다다음 주
dadaeum ju

in February
이월에
iwore

in 2018
2018년에
icheonsippallyeone

in the '80s
80년대에
palsimnyeondaee

What day is it?
무슨 요일이에요?
museun yoirieyo

What is today's date?
오늘이
며칠이에요?
oneuri myeochirieyo

spring
봄
bom

summer
여름
yeoreum

autumn
가을
gaeul

winter
겨울
gyeoul

in spring
봄에
bome

in winter
겨울에
gyeoure

How's the weather?
날씨가 어때요?
nalssiga eottaeyo

What's the forecast for today/tomorrow?
오늘/내일 일기예보가 어때요?
oneul/naeil ilgiyeboga eottaeyo

Is it going to rain?
비가 내릴까요?
biga naerilkkayo

What a lovely day!
날씨가 정말 좋아요!
nalssiga jeongmal joayo

What awful weather!
날씨가 정말 나빠요!
nalssiga jeongmal nappayo

It's sunny.
날이 맑아요.
nari malgayo

It's cloudy.
날이 흐려요.
nari heuryeoyo

It's misty.
안개가 꼈어요.
angaega kkyeosseoyo

It's foggy/stormy.
안개가 짙게 꼈어요/
비바람이 몰아쳐요.
angaega jitge kkyeosseoyo/
bibarami morachyeoyo

It's freezing.
너무 추워요.
neomu chuwoyo

It's raining/snowing.
비가/눈이 와요.
biga/nuni wayo

It's windy.
바람이 불어요.
barami bureoyo

It is...
날씨가...
nalssiga...

nice
좋아요
joayo

hot
더워요
deowoyo

warm
따뜻해요
ttatteutaeyo

cool
선선해요
seonseonhaeyo

wet
비가 와요
biga wayo

humid
습해요
seupaeyo

mild
포근해요
pogeunhaeyo

hail
우박
ubak

ice
얼음
eoreum

gale
강풍
gangpung

thunder
천둥
cheondung

lightning
번개
beongae

TRANSPORT | 교통

Korea has an excellent public transport system with extensive networks of railways, highways, bus routes, and air routes throughout the country. Major cities such as Seoul and Busan have good, modern underground systems, and other cities are catching up. However, roads are very busy on weekdays with people who commute to work.

helicopter
헬리콥터
hellikopteo

rotor
로터헤드
roteohedeu

blade
회전 날개
hoejeon nalgae

cockpit
조종석
jojongseok

nose
기수
gisu

tail
후미
humi

YOU MIGHT SAY...

Excuse me...
실례합니다...
sillyehamnida...

Where is...?
... 어디에 있어요?
... eodie isseoyo

What's the quickest way to...?
... 에 가는 가장 빠른 길이
어디예요?
... e ganeun gajang ppareun giri
eodiyeyo

Is it far from here?
여기에서 멀어요?
yeogieseo meoreoyo

I'm lost.
길을 잃었어요.
gireul ireosseoyo

Can I walk there?
거기까지 걸어갈 수 있어요?
geogikkaji georeogal su isseoyo

Is there a bus/train to...?
... 로 가는 버스가/기차가
있어요?
... ro ganeun beoseuga/gichaga
isseoyo

A single/return ticket, please.
편도/왕복 표 주세요.
pyeondo/wangbok pyo juseyo

YOU MIGHT HEAR...

It's over there.
저기예요.
jeogiyeyo

It's in the other direction.
다른 방향이에요.
dareun banghyangieyo

It's ... minutes away.
... 분 거리에 있어요.
... bun georie isseoyo

Go straight ahead.
똑바로 가세요.
ttokbaro gaseyo

Turn left/right.
왼쪽으로/오른쪽으로
도세요.
oenjjogeuro/oreunjjogeuro doseyo

It's next to/near to...
... 옆이에요/근처예요.
... yeopieyo/geuncheoyeyo

It's opposite...
... 반대편이에요.
... bandaepyeonieyo

Follow the signs for...
... 표시를 따라가세요.
... pyosireul ttaragaseyo

VOCABULARY

street 길 gil	traffic jam 교통 체증 gyotong chejeung	route 경로 gyeongno
commuter 통근자 tonggeunja	rush hour 출퇴근 시간 chultoegeun sigan	to walk 걷다 geotda
driver 운전자 unjeonja	public transport 대중교통 daejunggyotong	to drive 운전하다 unjeonhada
passenger 승객 seunggaek	taxi 택시 taeksi	to turn 돌다 dolda
pedestrian 보행자 bohaengja	taxi rank 택시 승차장 taeksi seungchajang	to commute 통근하다 tonggeunhada
traffic 교통 gyotong	directions 방향 banghyang	to take a taxi 택시를 타다 taeksireul tada

YOU SHOULD KNOW...

At pedestrian crossings in Korea, it is illegal to cross the road when the red light is showing even if there is no traffic.

map
지도
jido

road sign
표지판
pyojipan

timetable
시간표
siganpyo

Traffic drives on the right-hand side in Korea. To be allowed to drive, you must obtain an international driving permit before you arrive in the country, and you will need to show it to rent a car.

YOU MIGHT SAY...

Is this the road to...?
이 길이 ... 로 가는
길이에요?
i giri ... ro ganeun girieyo

Can I park here?
여기에 주차해도 돼요?
yeogie juchahaedo dwaeyo

Do I have to pay to park?
주차하려면 돈 내야 해요?
juchaharyeomyeon don naeya haeyo

Where can I hire a car?
어디에서 차를 렌트할 수
있어요?
eodieseo chareul renteuhal su isseoyo

I'd like to hire a car...
... 차를 렌트하고 싶어요.
... chareul renteuhago sipeoyo

... for four days.
나흘 동안...
naheul dongan...

... for a week.
일주일 동안...
iljuil dongan...

What is the daily/weekly rate?
하루에/일주일에 얼마예요?
harue/iljuire eolmayeyo

When/Where must I return it?
언제/어디에 반납해야
돼요?
eonje/eodie bannapaeya dwaeyo

Where is the nearest petrol station?
가장 가까운 주유소가
어디예요?
gajang gakkaun juyusoga eodiyeyo

I'd like ... won of fuel, please.
... 원어치 넣어 주세요.
... woneochi neoeo juseyo

I'd like ... litres of fuel, please.
... 리터 넣어 주세요.
... riteo neoeo juseyo

It's pump number...
... 번 주유기예요.
... beon juyugiyeyo

You can/can't park here.
여기에 주차 해도 돼요/하면
안 돼요.
yeogie jucha haedo dwaeyo/hamyeon
an dwaeyo

It's free to park here.
주차가 무료예요.
juchaga muryoyeyo

Car hire is ... per day.
차 렌트는 하루에 ...
원이에요.
cha renteuneun harue ... wonieyo

May I see your documents, please?
서류를 보여 주시겠어요?
seoryureul boyeo jusigesseoyo

Please return it to...
... 로 반납해 주세요.
... ro bannapae juseyo

Please return the car with a full
tank of fuel.
기름을 다 채워서 반납해
주세요.
gireumeul da chaewoseo bannapae
juseyo

Which pump are you at?
몇 번 주유기예요?
myeot beon juyugiyeyo

How much fuel would you like?
얼마나 넣어 드릴까요?
eolmana neoeo deurilkkayo

VOCABULARY

people carrier
승합차
seunghapcha

caravan
캠핑 트레일러
kaemping teureilleo

motorhome
캠핑카
kaempingka

passenger seat
조수석
josuseok

driver's seat
운전석
unjeonseok

back seat
뒷자석
dwitjaseok

child seat
카시트
kasiteu

sunroof
선루프
seollupeu

engine
엔진
enjin

automatic
자동변속기 차량
jadongbyeonsokgi
charyang

electric
전기
jeongi

hybrid
하이브리드
haibeurideu

battery	fuel tank	to park
배터리	연료 탱크	주차하다
baeteori	yeollyo taengkeu	juchahada
brake	gearbox	to reverse
브레이크	기어 박스	후진하다
beureikeu	gieo bakseu	hujinhada
accelerator	Breathalyser®	to slow down
액셀	음주 측정기	속도를 줄이다
aeksel	eumju cheukjeonggi	sokdoreul jurida
air conditioning	transmission	to speed
에어컨	변속기	속도를 높이다
eeokeon	byeonsokgi	sokdoreul nopida
clutch	to brake	to start the engine
클러치	감속하다	시동을 걸다
keulleochi	gamsokada	sidongeul geolda
exhaust (pipe)	to overtake	to stop
배기관	추월하다	멈추다
baegigwan	chuwolhada	meomchuda

YOU SHOULD KNOW...

In Korea, all motorways are toll roads. You can obtain an electric tag called a Hi-Pass, which allows you to pay contactless without stopping at a toll gate.

INTERIOR

dashboard
계기판
gyegipan

fuel gauge
연료계
yeollyogye

gear stick
변속 레버
byeonsok rebeo

glove compartment
글로브박스
geullobeubakseu

handbrake
핸드 브레이크
haendeu beureikeu

headrest
머리 받침대
meori batchimdae

ignition
시동장치
sidongjangchi

rearview mirror
백미러
baengmireo

sat nav
내비게이션
naebigeisyeon

seatbelt
안전벨트
anjeonbelteu

speedometer
속도계
sokdogye

steering wheel
핸들
haendeul

boot
트렁크
teureongkeu

roof
지붕
jibung

door
문
mun

window
창문
changmun

wing
펜더
pendeo

wheel
바퀴
bakwi

tyre
타이어
taieo

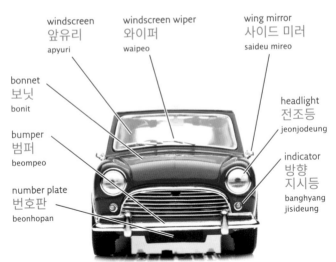

windscreen
앞유리
apyuri

windscreen wiper
와이퍼
waipeo

wing mirror
사이드 미러
saideu mireo

bonnet
보닛
bonit

bumper
범퍼
beompeo

number plate
번호판
beonhopan

headlight
전조등
jeonjodeung

indicator
방향
지시등
banghyang
jisideung

In Korea, foreign visitors can only drive if they have an international driving licence.

VOCABULARY

corner 모퉁이 motungi	diversion 우회로 uhoero	car insurance 자동차 보험 jadongcha boheom
exit 출구 chulgu	roadworks 도로 공사 doro gongsa	car hire/rental 렌터카 renteoka
slip road 진입로 jinimno	parking meter 주차권 발매기 juchagwon balmaegi	unleaded petrol 무연 휘발유 muyeon hwiballyu
layby 차량 일시 대피소 charyang ilsi daepiso	driving licence 운전면허증 unjeonmyeonheojeung	diesel 디젤유 dijeryu
speed limit 제한 속도 jehan sokdo	car registration document 자동차 등록증 jadongcha deungnokjeung	charging point 충전소 chungjeonso

YOU SHOULD KNOW...

Speed limits on Korean roads go by kmph, not mph. The speed limits for different types of roads are:

motorways – 100 kmph

1st grade roads – 80 kmph

2nd grade roads – 60 kmph.

There is also a lower limit which is 50 kmph for motorways.

bridge
다리
dari

car park
주차장
juchajang

car wash
세차장
sechajang

fuel pump
주유기
juyugi

junction
분기점
bungijeom

kerb
연석
yeonseok

lane
차선
chaseon

motorway
고속 도로
gosok doro

parking space
주차 공간
jucha gonggan

pavement
인도
indo

petrol station
주유소
juyuso

pothole
구덩이
gudeongi

road
도로
doro

speed camera
속도 감시 카메라
sokdo gamsi kamera

ticket machine
표 판매기
pyo panmaegi

toll point
톨게이트
tolgeiteu

traffic cone
원뿔 표지판
wonppul pyojipan

traffic lights
신호등
sinhodeung

traffic warden
주차 단속원
jucha dansogwon

tunnel
터널
teoneol

zebra crossing
횡단보도
hoengdangbodo

CAR TROUBLE | 차량 고장

If you break down on the motorway, call either the police or your insurance company who should be able to arrange to have you towed. If you have an accident, call the police on 112 or the ambulance/fire service on 119.

YOU MIGHT SAY...

Can you help me?
저 좀 도와주실 수 있어요?
jeo jom dowajusil su isseoyo

I've broken down.
차가 고장났어요.
chaga gojangnasseoyo

I've had an accident.
사고를 당했어요.
sagoreul danghaesseoyo

I've run out of petrol.
연료가 떨어졌어요.
yeollyoga tteoreojyeosseoyo

I've got a flat tyre.
타이어가 펑크났어요.
taieoga peongkeunasseoyo

I've lost my car keys.
차 열쇠를 잃어버렸어요.
cha yeolsoereul ireobeoryeosseoyo

The car won't start.
차 시동이 안 걸려요.
cha sidongi an geollyeoyo

I've been injured.
제가 다쳤어요.
jega dachyeosseoyo

Call an ambulance.
구급차를 부르세요.
gugeupchareul bureuseyo

Can you send a breakdown van?
견인차 보내주실 수 있어요?
gyeonincha bonaejusil su isseoyo

Is there a garage/petrol station nearby?
정비소가/주유소가 근처에 있어요?
jeongbisoga/juyusoga geuncheoe isseoyo

Can you help me change this wheel?
이 바퀴 바꾸는 걸 도와주실 수 있어요?
i bakwi bakkuneun geol dowajusil su isseoy

How much will a repair cost?
수리비용이 얼마일까요?
suribiyongi eolmailkkayo

When will the car be fixed?
언제 수리가 될까요?
eonje suriga doelkkayo

YOU MIGHT HEAR...

Do you need any help?
도와드릴까요?
dowadeurilkkayo

Are you hurt?
다치셨어요?
dachisyeosseoyo

What's wrong with your car?
차에 무슨 문제가 있어요?
chae museun munjega isseoyo

Where have you broken down?
어디에서 고장났어요?
eodieseo gojangnasseoyo

I can give you a jumpstart.
제가 부스터 케이블로
도와드릴 수 있어요.
jega buseuteo keibeullo dowadeuril su
isseoyo

The repairs will cost...
수리비는 ... 원이에요.
suribineun ... wonieyo

We need to order new parts.
새 부품을 주문해야 돼요.
sae bupumeul jumunhaeya dwaeyo

The car will be ready by...
... 까지 준비될 거예요.
... kkaji junbidoel geoyeyo

I need your insurance details.
보험 정보가 필요해요.
boheom jeongboga piryohaeyo

Do you have your driving licence?
운전면허증 있어요?
unjeonmyeonheojeung isseoyo

VOCABULARY

accident
사고
sago

breakdown
고장
gojang

collision
충돌 사고
chungdol sago

flat tyre
타이어 펑크
taieo peongkeu

mechanic
정비공
jeongbigong

car insurance
자동차 보험
jadongcha boheom

to break down
고장나다
gojangnada

to have an accident
사고를 당하다
sagoreul danghada

to have a flat tyre
타이어에 펑크가
나다
taieoe peongkeuga nada

to change a tyre
타이어를
교체하다
taieoreul gyochehada

to tow
끌다
kkeulda

to repair
수리하다
surihada

GENERAL

airbag
에어백
eeobaek

antifreeze
부동액
budongaek

garage
정비소
jeongbiso

jack
잭
jaek

jump leads
부스터 케이블
buseuteo keibeul

snow chains
스노체인
seunochein

spare wheel
스페어타이어
seupeeotaieo

tow truck
견인차
gyeonincha

warning triangle
안전 삼각대
anjeon samgakdae

Local bus services are often well organized and useful for short trips; for longer journeys, rail services are usually faster and more frequent. However, long-distance coaches are much cheaper than trains.

YOU MIGHT SAY...

Is there a bus to...?
... 에 가는 버스 있어요?
... e ganeun beoseu isseoyo

When is the next bus to...?
... 에 가는 다음 버스가 언제예요?
... e ganeun daeum beoseuga eonjeyeyo

Which bus goes to the city centre?
시내로 가는 버스가 몇 번이에요?
sinaero ganeun beoseuga myeot beonieyo

Where is the bus stop?
버스 정류장이 어디에 있어요?
beoseu jeongnyujangi eodie isseoyo

Which stand does the coach leave from?
어느 탑승장에서 그 버스가 출발해요?
eoneu tapseungjangeseo geu beoseuga chulbalhaeyo

Where can I buy tickets?
표는 어디에서 사요?
pyoneun eodieseo sayo

How much is it to go to...?
... 에 가는 버스가 얼마예요?
... e ganeun beoseuga eolmayeyo

A full/half fare, please.
성인표/어린이표 주세요.
seonginpyo/eorinipyo juseyo

Could you tell me when to get off?
내려야 될 때 알려주실 수 있어요?
naeryeoya doel ttae allyeojusil su isseoyo

How many stops is it?
몇 정거장 가요?
myeot jeonggeojang gayo

I want to get off at the next stop, please.
다음 정류장에서 내리려고요.
daeum jeongnyujangeseo naeriryeogoyo

YOU SHOULD KNOW...

In most Korean cities, people must get on the bus at the front door and get off at the back door.

The number 17 goes to...
17번 버스는 ... 에 가요.
sipchilbeon beoseuneun ... e gayo

You can/can't buy the tickets on the bus.
버스 안에서 승차권을 살 수 있어요/없어요.
beoseu aneseo seungchagwoneul sal su isseoyo/eopseoyo

The bus stop is down the road.
그 버스 정류장은 길 따라 저쪽에 있어요.
geu beoseu jeongnyujangeun gil ttara jeojjoge isseoyo

You buy tickets at the office.
매표소에서 표를 사세요.
maepyosoeseo pyoreul saseyo

It leaves from stand 21.
21번 탑승장에서 출발해요.
isibilbeon tapseungjangeseo chulbalhaeyo

VOCABULARY

bus lane
버스 전용 차선
beoseu jeonyong chaseon

bus stop
버스 정류장
beoseu jeongnyujang

shuttle bus
셔틀버스
syeoteulbeoseu

bus pass
버스 정기권
beoseu jeonggigwon

fare
요금
yogeum

school bus
스쿨버스
seukulbeoseu

bus station
버스 터미널
beoseu teomineol

concession
할인
harin

to catch the bus
버스를 잡아타다
beoseureul jabatada

bus
버스
beoseu

coach
대형 버스
daehyeong beoseu

minibus
소형 버스
sohyeong beoseu

If you wish to ride a motorbike in Korea, you can swap your own driving licence for a temporary Korean one. This will allow you to ride a 125cc motorbike. For anything more powerful, you will need a special motorbike licence.

VOCABULARY

motorcyclist
오토바이를 타는
사람
otobaireul taneun saram

moped
모페드
mopedeu

scooter
스쿠터
seukuteo

fuel tank
연료 탱크
yeollyo taengkeu

handlebars
핸들
haendeul

headlight
전조등
jeonjodeung

mudguard
흙받기
heukbatgi

kickstand
받침다리
batchimdari

exhaust pipe
배기관
baegigwan

boots
부츠
bucheu

crash helmet
헬멧
helmet

helmet cam
헬멧에 다는 카메라
helmese daneun kamera

leather gloves
가죽장갑
gajukjanggap

leather jacket
가죽점퍼
gajukjeompeo

motorbike
오토바이
otobai

Bicycles are widely used in Korea and can be hired in many tourist areas through a "Public bike sharing" system. This allows people to rent a bike through a mobile phone app, paying very little and returning the bikes to any stand.

YOU MIGHT SAY...

Where can I hire a bicycle?
자전거 대여하는 곳은
어디예요?
jajeongeo daeyeohaneun goseun
eodiyeyo

How much is it to hire?
자전거 빌리는 데 얼마예요?
jajeongeo billineun de eolmayeyo

My bike has a puncture.
제 자전거에 펑크가 났어요.
je jajeongeoe peongkeuga nasseoyo

YOU MIGHT HEAR...

Bike hire is ... per day/week.
자전거 대여는 하루에/
일주일에 ... 원이에요.
jajeongeo daeyeoneun harue/iljuire ...
wonieyo

You must wear a helmet.
헬멧을 써야 해요.
helmeseul sseoya haeyo

There is a cycle path.
자전거 도로가 있어요.
jajeongeo doroga isseoyo

VOCABULARY

cyclist
자전거 타는 사람
jajeongeo taneun saram

mountain bike
산악 자전거
sanak jajeongeo

road bike
로드 바이크
rodeu baikeu

rental/hire
대여
daeyeo

rental place
대여소
daeyeoso

bike stand
자전거 거치대
jajeongeo geochidae

child seat
유아 안장
yua anjang

cycle lane/path
자전거 도로/길
jajeongeo doro/gil

to cycle
자전거를 타다
jajeongeoreul tada

YOU SHOULD KNOW...

Wearing a helmet is compulsory in Korea.

ACCESSORIES

bell
벨
bel

bike lock
자전거 자물쇠
jajeongeo jamulsoe

front light
전조등
jeonjodeung

helmet
헬멧
helmet

pump
공기 펌프
gonggi peompeu

reflector
후미등
humideung

BICYCLE

brake
브레이크
beureikeu

handlebars
핸들
haendeul

gears
기어
gieo

crossbar
탑 튜브
tap tyubeu

saddle
안장
anjang

frame
시트 튜브
siteu tyubeu

wheel
바퀴
bakwi

chain
체인
chein

tyre
타이어
taieo

pedal
페달
pedal

RAIL TRAVEL | 기차여행

The Korean railway system has an extensive network operated by KORAIL, and is the best option for long-distance travel. The fares depend on the type of train and how far you travel. There is also a Korail pass 코레일 패스 (koreil paeseu) which is a rail pass exclusively for foreigners and allows unlimited use of all trains, including the bullet train, KTX.

YOU MIGHT SAY...

Is there a train to...?
... 에 가는 기차가 있어요?
... e ganeun gichaga isseoyo

When is the next train to...?
... 에 가는 다음 기차가 언제예요?
... e ganeun daeum gichaga eonjeyeyo

Which platform does it leave from?
어느 승강장에서 출발해요?
eoneu seunggangjangeseo chulbalhaeyo

A ticket to..., please.
... 에 가는 표 한 장 주세요.
... e ganeun pyo han jang juseyo

I'd like to reserve a seat/couchette, please.
좌석 하나/침대자리 하나 예약하고 싶어요.
jwaseok hana/chimdaejari hana yeyakago sipeoyo

I would like to buy a Korail pass, please.
코레일 패스 하나 주세요.
koreil paeseu hana juseyo

How many days is this pass valid for?
며칠 동안 사용할 수 있어요?
myeochil dongan sayonghal su isseoyo

Do I have to change?
환승해야 해요?
hwanseunghaeya haeyo

Where do I change for...?
... 에 가려면 어디에서 환승해요?
... e garyeomyeon eodieseo hwanseunghaeyo

Where is platform 4?
4번 승강장이 어디예요?
sabeon seunggangjangi eodiyeyo

Is this the right platform for...?
여기가 ... 에 가는 승강장 맞아요?
yeogiga ... e ganeun seunggangjang majayo

Is this the train for...?
이게 ... 에 가는 기차가 맞아요?
ige ... e ganeun gichaga majayo

Is this seat free?
여기 자리 비었어요?
yeogi jari bieosseoyo

I've missed my train!
기차를 놓쳤어요!
gichareul nochyeosseoyo

YOU MIGHT HEAR...

The next train leaves at...
다음 기차는 ... 시에
출발해요.
daeum gichaneun ... sie chulbalhaeyo

Would you like a single or return
ticket?
편도 사시겠어요, 아니면
왕복 사시겠어요?
pyeondo sasigesseoyo, animyeon
wangbok sasigesseoyo

Would you like a first-class or a
standard-class ticket?
특실 하시겠어요, 아니면
일반실 하시겠어요?
teuksil hasigesseoyo, animyeon
ilbansil hasigesseoyo

The pass is valid for 3 days/5 days.
패스는 3일권/5일권이에요.
paeseuneun samilgwon/oilgwonieyo

I'm sorry, this journey is fully booked.
죄송합니다만, 그 기차표는
매진됐어요.
joesonghamnidaman, geu gichapyoneun
maejindwaesseoyo

You must change at...
... 에서 환승해야 해요.
... eseo hwanseunghaeya haeyo

Platform 4 is down there.
4번 승강장은 아래쪽에
있어요.
sabeon seunggangjangeun araejjoge
isseoyo

This is the right train/platform.
이 기차가/승강장이 맞아요.
i gichaga/seunggangjangi majayo

You have to go to platform 2.
2번 승강장으로 가셔야 해요.
ibeon seunggangjangeuro gasyeoya
haeyo

This seat is free/taken.
여기 자리 비었어요/다른
사람이 있어요.
yeogi jari bieosseoyo/dareun sarami
isseoyo

The restaurant car is in coach 3.
식당칸은 3호차예요.
sikdangkaneun samhochayeyo

The next stop is...
다음 정류장은 ... 입니다.
daeum jeongnyujangeun ... imnida

Change here for...
... 에 가시는 분은 이곳에서
환승하시기 바랍니다.
... e gasineun buneun igoseseo
hwanseunghasigi baramnida

VOCABULARY

passenger train
여객 열차
yeogaek yeolcha

guard
경비원
gyeongbiwon

single ticket
편도표
pyeondopyo

freight train
화물 열차
hwamul yeolcha

line
선로
seollo

first-class
특별실
teukbyeolsil

coach
객차
gaekcha

metro station
지하철 역
jihacheol yeok

standard-class
일반실
ilbansil

porter
철도 승무원
cheoldo seungmuwon

left luggage
수하물 보관소
suhamul bogwanso

to change trains
기차를 환승하다
gichareul hwanseunghada

carriage
객차
gaekcha

couchette
침대 객실
chimdae gaeksil

departure board
출발 안내 전광판
chulbal annae jeongwangpan

KTX
고속열차
gosogyeolcha

light railway
경전철
gyeongjeoncheol

locomotive
기관차
gigwancha

luggage rack
선반
seonban

metro
지하철
jihacheol

platform
승강장
seunggangjang

restaurant car
식당칸
sikdangkan

signal box
신호소
sinhoso

ticket
표
pyo

ticket barrier
개찰구
gaechalgu

ticket machine
표 판매기
pyo panmaegi

ticket office
매표소
maepyoso

track
선로
seollo

train
기차
gicha

train station
기차역
gichayeok

There are 8 airports offering international flights in Korea, as well as 7 airports that provide domestic air routes.

YOU MIGHT SAY...

I'm looking for check-in/my gate.
탑승 수속대를/탑승구를
찾고 있어요.
tapseung susokdaereul/
tapseunggureul chatgo isseoyo

I'm checking in one case.
가방 한 개 부치려고요.
gabang han gae buchiryeogoyo

Which gate does the plane leave from?
몇 번 탑승구에서 비행기가
출발해요?
myeot beon tapseunggueseo
bihaenggiga chulbalhaeyo

When does the gate open/close?
탑승구는 언제 열어요/닫아요?
tapseungguneun eonje yeoreoyo/dadayo

Is the flight on time?
비행기가 정시에
운항하나요?
bihaenggiga jeongsie unhanghanayo

I would like a window seat/an aisle seat, please.
창가 자리/복도 자리에 앉고
싶어요.
changga jari/bokdo jarie ango sipeoyo

I've lost my luggage.
제 수하물 가방을
잃어버렸어요.
je suhamul gabangeul ireobeoryeosseoyo

My flight has been delayed.
제 비행기가 연착됐어요.
je bihaenggiga yeonchakdwaesseoyo

I've missed my connecting flight.
제 연결 항공편을 놓쳤어요.
je yeongyeol hanggongpyeoneul
nochyeosseoyo

Is there a shuttle bus service?
셔틀버스가 있어요?
syeoteulbeoseuga isseoyo

YOU MIGHT HEAR...

Check-in has opened for flight...
... 행 비행기 탑승 수속을
시작합니다.
... haeng bihaenggi tapseung susogeul
sijakamnida

May I see your ticket/passport?
탑승권을/여권을
보여주시겠어요?
tapseunggwoneul/yeogwoneul
boyeojusigesseoyo

How many bags are you checking in?
수하물은 몇 개 부치세요?
suhamureun myeot gae buchiseyo

Is this your bag?
이거 고객님 가방인가요?
igeo gogaengnim gabangingayo

Please go to gate number...
... 번 탑승구로 가시기
바랍니다.
... beon tapseungguro gasigi baramnida

Flight ... is now ready for boarding.
항공편 ... 탑승을
시작하겠습니다.
hanggongpyeon ... tapseungeul sijakagetseumnida

Your flight is on time/delayed/
cancelled.
비행기가 정시에
운항합니다/연착됐습니다/
취소됐습니다.
bihaenggiga jeongsie unhanghamnida/
yeonchakdwaetseumnida/
chwisodwaetseumnida

Last call for passenger...
... 편 항공기 탑승객들께
마지막으로 안내드립니다.
... pyeon hanggonggi
tapseunggaekdeulkke majimageuro
annaedeurimnida

VOCABULARY

airline
항공사
hanggongsa

customs
세관
segwan

seatbelt
안전벨트
anjeonbelteu

flight
항공편
hanggongpyeon

cabin crew
승무원
seungmuwon

tray table
간이 탁자
gani takja

Arrivals/Departures
도착/출발
dochak/chulbal

business class
비지니스 클래스
bijiniseu keullaeseu

overhead locker
좌석 위 선반
jwaseok wi seonban

security
보안
boan

economy class
이코노미 클래스
ikonomi keullaeseu

wing
날개
nalgae

passport control
출입국 심사대
churipguk simsadae

aisle
통로
tongno

fuselage
기체
giche

engine
엔진
enjin

hand luggage
휴대 수하물
hyudae suhamul

connecting flight
연결 항공편
yeongyeol
hanggongpyeon

hold
화물칸
hwamulkan

cabin baggage
기내 수하물
ginae suhamul

jetlag
시차로 인한 피로
sicharo inhan piro

hold luggage
위탁 수하물
witak suhamul

excess baggage
초과 수하물
chogwa suhamul

to check in (online)
(온라인) 탑승 수속
(ollain) tapseung susok

aeroplane
항공기
hanggonggi

airport
공항
gonghang

baggage reclaim
수하물 찾는 곳
suhamul channeun got

boarding card
탑승권
tapseunggwon

cabin
기내
ginae

check-in desk
탑승 수속 창구
tapseung susok changgu

cockpit
조종석
jojongseok

duty-free shop
면세점
myeonsejeom

holdall
큰 손가방
keun songabang

information board
안내판
annaepan

luggage trolley
수하물 카트
suhamul kateu

passport
여권
yeogwon

pilot
조종사
jojongsa

runway
활주로
hwaljuro

suitcase
여행 가방
yeohaeng gabang

terminal
터미널
teomineol

Long-distance ferries link Korea to China and Japan, while local ferries serve Jeju Island and other small islands.

YOU MIGHT SAY...

When is the next boat to...?
... 에 가는 다음 배가
언제예요?
... e ganeun daeum baega eonjeyeyo

Where does the boat leave from?
배가 어디에서 출발해요?
baega eodieseo chulbalhaeyo

What time is the last boat to...?
... 에 가는 마지막 배가
언제예요?
... e ganeun majimak baega eonjeyeyo

How long is the trip/crossing?
배 타고 가는데 얼마나
걸려요?
bae tago ganeunde eolmana geollyeoyo

How many crossings a day are there?
가는 배가 하루에 몇 번
있어요?
ganeun baega harue myeot beon isseoyo

How much is it for ... passengers/ a vehicle?
... 명에/차량 한 대에
얼마예요?
... myeonge/charyang han daee eolmayeyo

I feel seasick.
뱃멀미가 나요.
baenmeolmiga nayo

YOU MIGHT HEAR...

The boat leaves from...
배는 ... 에서 출발해요.
baeneun ... eseo chulbalhaeyo

The trip/crossing lasts...
가는데 ... 걸려요.
ganeunde ... geollyeoyo

There are ... crossings a day.
하루에 ... 번 있어요.
harue ... beon isseoyo

The ferry is delayed/cancelled.
운항이 지연/취소 됐어요.
unhangi jiyeon/chwiso dwaesseoyo

Sea conditions are good/bad.
해상 상태가 좋아요/나빠요.
haesang sangtaega joayo/nappayo

46

ferry 연락선 yeollakseon	harbour 항만 hangman	crew 선원 seonwon
ferry crossing 연락선 도항 yeollakseon dohang	port 항구 hanggu	to board 승선하다 seungseonhada
ferry terminal 배 선착장 bae seonchakjang	coastguard 해안 경비대 haean gyeongbidae	to sail 항해하다 hanghaehada
car deck 차량용 갑판 charyangyong gappan	captain 선장 seonjang	to dock 부두에 대다 budue daeda

GENERAL

anchor
닻
dat

buoy
부표
bupyo

gangway
트랩
teuraep

jetty
선창
seonchang

lifebuoy
구명튜브
gumyeongtyubeu

lifejacket
구명조끼
gumyeongjokki

FERRY

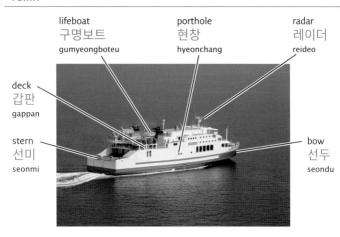

lifeboat
구명보트
gumyeongboteu

porthole
현창
hyeonchang

radar
레이더
reideo

deck
갑판
gappan

stern
선미
seonmi

bow
선두
seondu

OTHER BOATS

canal boat
운하선
unhaseon

inflatable dinghy
고무 보트
gomu boteu

liner
정기선
jeonggiseon

sailing boat
돛단배
dotdanbae

trawler
투망어선
tumangeoseon

yacht
요트
yoteu

IN THE HOME | 주거생활

Korea attracts huge numbers of tourists and expats looking for a place to call their "home" for a time, whether it's for a holiday or for a longer-term stay. This could be a central city flat or communal living in a hostel or guest house.

block of flats
아파트
apateu

roof
지붕
jibung

balcony
베란다
beranda

window
창문
changmun

Most of Korea's population lives in urban areas. The most common type of residential building in Korea is an apartment block, usually within a complex 단지 (danji) and built by the same developer.

YOU MIGHT SAY...

I live in.../I'm staying at...
... 에서 살아요/지내요.
... eseo sarayo/jinaeyo

My address is...
제 집 주소는 ... 이에요/예요.
je jib jusoneun ... ieyo/yeyo

I have a flat/house.
아파트 한 채/주택 한 채
있어요.
apateu han chae/jutaek han chae isseoyo

I'm the homeowner/tenant.
제가 집주인이에요/
세입자예요.
jega jibjuinieyo/seipjayeyo

I'd like to buy/rent a property here.
여기에서 집을 사고 싶어요/
임대하고 싶어요.
yeogieseo jibeul sago sipeoyo/
imdaehago sipeoyo

YOU MIGHT HEAR...

Where do you live?
어디에 사세요?
eodie saseyo

Where are you staying?
어디에서 지내세요?
eodieseo jinaeseyo

How long have you lived here?
얼마동안 여기에 살았어요?
eormana yeogie sarasseoyo

Are you the owner/tenant?
집주인이세요/세입자세요?
jipjuiniseyo/seibjaseyo

VOCABULARY

building	address	suburb
건물	주소	교외
geonmul	juso	gyowae

estate agent **부동산 중개인** budongsan junggaein	neighbour **이웃** iut	to rent **임대하다** imdaehada
landlord/landlady **집주인** jibjuin	mortgage **주택 담보 대출** jutaek dambo daechul	to own **소유하다** soyuhada
tenant **세입자** seibja	rent **집세** jipse	to move house **이사하다** isahada

---

YOU SHOULD KNOW...

In Korea, there is a unique system when renting property, called "Jeonse (전세)". The tenant pays a large deposit, about 50-70% of the market value of the property, but does not pay monthly rent. The landlord pays the whole deposit back to the tenant at the end of the contract.

bungalow
방갈로
banggallo

courtyard house
중정형주택
jungjeonghyeongjeotaek

detached house
단독주택
dandokjutaek

high-rise block
고층아파트
gocheungapateu

studio flat
원룸
wollum

villa
저택
jeotaek

As well as apartment blocks, you will find detached houses and villas in Korea; these are either in big cities owned by the very wealthy, or in the affluent countryside where farmers build their own properties.

YOU MIGHT SAY...

There's a problem with...
... 에 문제가 있어요.
... e munjega isseoyo

It's not working.
고장났어요.
gojangnasseoyo

The drains are blocked.
배수구가 막혔어요.
baesugu makyeosseoyo

The boiler has broken.
보일러가 고장났어요.
boilleoga gojangnasseoyo

There's no hot water.
뜨거운 물이 안 나와요.
tteugeoun muri an nawayo

We have a power cut.
전기가 나갔어요.
jeongiga nagasseoyo

I need a plumber/an electrician.
배관공이/전기기술자가
필요해요.
baegwangongi/jeongigisuljaga piryohaeyo

Can you recommend anyone?
누구 추천해 줄 수 있어요?
nugu chucheonhae jul su isseoyo

Can it be repaired?
고칠 수 있을까요?
gochil su isseulkkayo

I can smell gas/smoke.
가스/연기 냄새가 나요.
gaseu/yeongi naemsaega nayo

YOU MIGHT HEAR...

How long has it been broken/leaking?
고장 난 지/물이 샌 지
얼마나 됐어요?
gojang nan ji/muri saen ji eolmana dwaesseoyo

Where is the electricity meter/water meter/fuse box?
전기 계량기/수도 계량기/
누전 차단기가 어디에 있어요?
jeongi gyeryanggi/sudo gyeryanggi/ nujeon chadangiga eodie isseoyo

VOCABULARY

room
방
bang

ceiling
천장
cheonjang

wall
벽
byeok

floor
바닥
badak

battery
건전지
geonjeonji

plug
플러그
peulleogeu

adaptor
어댑터
eodaepteo

socket
콘센트
konsenteu

extension cable
멀티탭
meoltitaep

electricity
전기
jeongi

air conditioning
에어컨
eeokeon

central heating
중앙난방
jungangnanbang

satellite dish
위성 안테나
wiseong antena

back door
뒷문
dwinmun

skylight
채광창
chaegwangchang

light bulb
전구
jeongu

to fix
고치다
gochida

to decorate
꾸미다
kkumida

INSIDE

boiler
보일러
boilleo

ceiling fan
천장 선풍기
cheonjang seonpunggi

fuse box
누전 차단기
nujeon chadangi

heater
난방기
nanbanggi

meter
계량기
gyeryanggi

radiator
라디에이터
radieiteo

security alarm
보안경보기
boangyeongbogi

smoke alarm
화재경보기
hwajaegyeongbogi

thermostat
온도 조절기
ondo jojeolgi

OUTSIDE

chimney
굴뚝
gulttuk

aerial
안테나
antena

gutter
홈통
homtong

drainpipe
배수관
baesugwan

roof
지붕
jibung

window
창문
changmun

driveway
입구
ipku

front door
현관문
hyeongwanmun

garage
차고
chago

YOU MIGHT SAY/HEAR...

Would you like to come round?
저희 집에 오시겠어요?
jeohi jibe osigesseoyo

May I come in?
들어가도 될까요?
deureogado doelkkayo

Hi! Come in.
안녕하세요! 들어오세요.
annyeonghaseyo! deureooseyo

Shall I take my shoes off?
신발 벗을까요?
sinbal beoseulkkayo

Make yourself at home.
편하게 계세요.
pyeonhage gyeseyo

Can I use your bathroom?
화장실 써도 될까요?
hwajangsil sseodo doelkkayo

Come round again soon.
조만간 또 오세요.
jomangan tto oseyo

Thanks for inviting me over.
초대해 줘서 고마워요.
chodaehae jwoseo gomawoyo

VOCABULARY

threshold/doorway
문지방
munjibang

console table
장식용 탁자
jangsigyong takja

to buzz somebody in
...에게 문을
열어주다
...ege muneul yeoreojuda

corridor
복도
bokdo

landing
층계참
cheunggyecham

to come in
들어오다
deureooda

hallway
현관
hyeongwan

staircase
계단
gyedan

to wipe one's feet
발을 닦다
bareul dakda

coat hook
벽걸이 후크
byeokgeori hukeu

banister
난간
nangan

to hang one's jacket up
겉옷을 걸다
geodoseul geolda

doorbell
초인종
choinjong

door handle
손잡이
sonjabi

doormat
도어매트
doeomaeteu

intercom
인터폰
inteopon

key
열쇠
yeolsoe

key fob
열쇠고리
yeolsoegori

lift
엘리베이터
ellibeiteo

shoe cupboard
신발장
sinbaljang

stairwell
계단실
gyedansil

VOCABULARY

vinyl flooring 비닐 바닥재 binil badakjae	footstool 발 받침대 bal batchimdae	radio 라디오 radio
underfloor heating 바닥 난방 badak nanbang	coffee table 탁자 takja	DVD/Blu-ray® player 디비디/블루레이 플레이어 dibidi/beullurei peulleieo
sofa bed 소파베드 sopabedeu	ornament 장식품 jangsikpum	remote control 리모컨 rimokeon
suite 가구 한 벌 gagu han beol	wall light 벽등 byeokdeung	to relax 편히 쉬다 pyeonhi swida
armchair 안락의자 allaguija	table lamp 탁상등 taksangdeung	to watch TV 티브이 보다 tibeui boda

YOU SHOULD KNOW...

Most Korean houses and flats have vinyl flooring and an underfloor heating system. Many people, therefore, like to sit on the floor, rather than on sofas and chairs.

GENERAL

bookcase 책장 chaekjang	 curtains 커튼 keoteun	 display cabinet 장식장 jangsikjang

TV
티브이
tibeui

TV stand
티브이 장식장
tibeui jangsikjang

Venetian blind
블라인드
beullaindeu

LOUNGE

picture
그림/사진
geurim/sajin

cushion
쿠션
kusyeon

wooden floor
마룻바닥
marutbadak

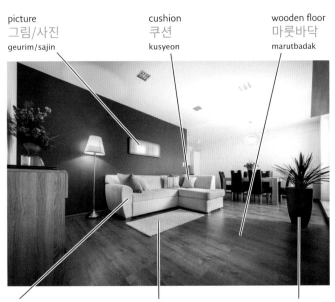

sofa
소파
sopa

rug
러그
reogeu

house plant
실내용 화초
sillaeyong hwacho

Nowadays, as in the UK, it is becoming more common for many Korean kitchens to feature a kitchen island.

VOCABULARY

kitchen island	to cook	to stir-fry
아일랜드 식탁	요리하다	볶다
aillaendeu siktak	yorihada	bokda

(electric) cooker	to boil	to steam
전기레인지	끓이다	찌다
jeongireinji	kkeurida	jjida

gas cooker	to fry	to wash up
가스레인지	튀기다	설거지하다
gaseureinji	twigida	seolgeojihada

YOU SHOULD KNOW...

The most important piece of equipment in a Korean kitchen is the electric rice cooker. Baking is not very popular in Korea although ovens are becoming more common.

MISCELLANEOUS ITEMS

aluminium foil
포일
poil

clingfilm
랩
raep

kitchen roll
키친타월
kichintawol

casserole dish
냄비
naembi

chopping board
도마
doma

colander
소쿠리
sokuri

cooker hood
후드
hudeu

electric rice cooker
전기밥솥
jeongibapsot

food processor
푸드 프로세서
pudeu peuroseseo

frying pan
프라이팬
peuraipaen

grater
강판
gangpan

kettle
주전자
jujeonja

kitchen knife
부엌칼
bueokkal

kitchen scales
주방용 저울
jubangyong jeoul

ladle
국자
gukja

measuring jug
계량컵
gyeryangkeop

pedal bin
페달 휴지통
pedal hyujitong

peeler
감자칼
gamjakal

pestle and mortar
절굿공이와 절구
jeolgutgongiwa jeolgu

rolling pin
밀대
mildae

saucepan
소스냄비
soseunaembi

sieve
체
che

spatula
뒤집개
dwijipgae

steamer
찜기
jjimgi

teapot
찻주전자
chatjujeonja

tin opener
통조림 따개
tongjorim ttagae

toaster
토스터
toseuteo

water cooler
정수기
jeongsugi

whisk
거품기
geopumgi

wooden spoon
나무 주걱
namu jugeok

KITCHEN

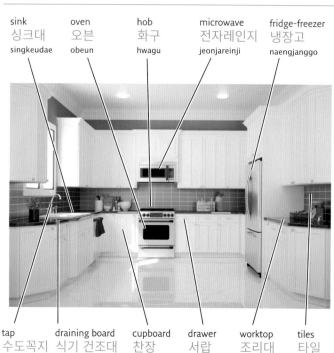

sink
싱크대
singkeudae

oven
오븐
obeun

hob
화구
hwagu

microwave
전자레인지
jeonjareinji

fridge-freezer
냉장고
naengjanggo

tap
수도꼭지
sudokkokji

draining board
식기 건조대
sikgi geonjodae

cupboard
찬장
chanjang

drawer
서랍
seorap

worktop
조리대
joridae

tiles
타일
tail

The kitchen and dining area are generally combined in Korean homes. People may invite close friends to their homes for a meal, but otherwise they generally prefer to invite people out to a restaurant.

YOU MIGHT SAY/HEAR...

Thank you for the meal I'm going to have.
잘 먹겠습니다.
jal meokgetseumnida

Thank you for the meal I had.
잘 먹었습니다.
jal meogeotseumnida

VOCABULARY

dining table 식탁 siktak	tablecloth 식탁보 siktakbo	to dine 식사하다 siksahada
sideboard 수납장 sunapjang	to set the table 밥상을 차리다 bapsangeul charida	to clear the table 밥상을 치우다 bapsangeul chiuda

YOU SHOULD KNOW...

Good table manners in Korea include: waiting for the most senior person at the table to start; not hitting the spoons or chopsticks on the bowl or standing them upright in the rice; and not standing up to reach a dish.

GENERAL

knife and fork
나이프와 포크
naipeuwa pokeu

Korean teacup
찻잔
chatjan

mug
머그잔
meogeujan

napkin
냅킨
naepkin

plate
접시
jeopsi

pot stand
냄비받침
naembibatchim

teaspoon
티스푼
tiseupun

tumbler
물잔
muljan

wine glass
와인잔
wainjan

TABLE SETTING

rice bowl
밥그릇
bapgeureut

soup bowl
국그릇
gukgeureut

spoon
숟가락
sutgarak

chopsticks
젓가락
jeotgarak

VOCABULARY

single bed 1인용 침대 irinyong chimdae	spare room 손님용 방 sonnimyong bang	to sleep 자다 jada
double bed 2인용 침대 iinyong chimdae	nursery 아기방 agibang	to wake up 일어나다 ireonada
bunk beds 2층 침대 icheung chimdae	headboard 침대 머리판 chimdae meoripan	to make the bed 침대를 정돈하다 chimdaereul jeongdonhada
master bedroom 안방 anbang	to go to bed 잠자리에 들다 jamjarie deulda	to change the sheets 시트를 갈다 siteureul galda

GENERAL

alarm clock
알람 시계
allam sigye

bedding
침구
chimgu

coat hanger
옷걸이
otgeori

dressing table
화장대
hwajangdae

laundry basket
빨래바구니
ppallaebaguni

sheets
침대시트
chimdaesiteu

mirror
거울
geoul

chest of drawers
서랍장
seorapjang

bed
침대
chimdae

wardrobe
옷장
otjang

duvet
이불
ibul

curtains
커튼
keoteun

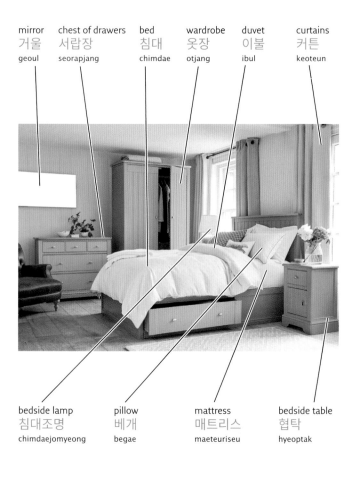

bedside lamp
침대조명
chimdaejomyeong

pillow
베개
begae

mattress
매트리스
maeteuriseu

bedside table
협탁
hyeoptak

THE BATHROOM | 욕실

Like in the UK, most Korean homes have the toilet in the bathroom. It is also quite common for there to be a drain in the bathroom floor in modern apartments. This allows people to wash down the whole bathroom when cleaning it.

VOCABULARY

shower curtain 샤워커튼 syawokeoteun	to have a bath/shower 목욕/샤워하다 mogyok/syawohada	to brush one's teeth 양치하다 yangchihada
toiletries 세면도구 semyeondogu	to wash one's hands 손을 씻다 soneul ssitda	to go to the toilet 화장실에 가다 hwajangsire gada

OTHER ITEMS

exfoliating glove
때수건
ttaesugeon

hairdryer
드라이기
deuraigi

plastic slippers
플라스틱 슬리퍼
peullaseutik seullipeo

shower puff
샤워볼
syawobol

soap
비누
binu

sponge
스폰지
seuponji

toilet brush
변기솔
byeongisol

toilet roll
화장지
hwajangji

towel
수건
sugeon

BATHROOM

mirror
거울
geoul

sink
세면대
semyeondae

shower
샤워기
syawogi

toilet
변기
byeongi

towel rail
수건걸이
sugeongeori

tap
수도꼭지
sudokkokji

cabinet
수납장
sunapjang

shower cubicle
샤워실
syawosil

bath
욕조
yokjo

Most Korean families live in apartment blocks and don't have their own garden. However, this doesn't stop them creating a green space at home, normally on the balcony.

VOCABULARY

flower 꽃 kkot	bird 새 sae	to water 물을 주다 mureul juda
weed 잡초 japcho	greenhouse 온실 onsil	to grow 키우다 kiuda
soil 흙 heuk	to weed 제초하다 jechohada	to plant 심다 simda

BALCONY

flowerpot stand 화분 진열대 hwabun jinyeoldae	shrub 관목 gwanmok	flowerpot 화분 hwabun	plant 화초 hwacho	decking 조립마루 jorimmaru

birdcage
새장
saejang

gardening gloves
원예용 장갑
wonyeyong janggap

trellis
격자울타리
gyeokjaultari

trowel
모종삽
mojongsap

watering can
물뿌리개
mulppurigae

weedkiller
제초제
jechoje

window box
창틀화분
changteulhwabun

VOCABULARY

utility room
다용도실
dayongdosil

household appliances
가전제품
gajeonjepum

dustbin
쓰레기통
sseuregitong

bleach
표백제
pyobaekje

disinfectant
살균제
salgyunje

washing-up liquid
주방 세제
jubang seje

to sweep the floor
바닥을 쓸다
badageul sseulda

to do the laundry
빨래하다
ppallaehada

to hoover
청소기로 청소하다
cheongsogiro cheongsohada

to tidy up
정리하다
jeongnihada

to clean
청소하다
cheongsohada

to take out the rubbish
쓰레기를 버리다
sseuregireul beorida

bin bag
쓰레기봉투
sseuregibongtu

brush
빗자루
bitjaru

bucket
양동이
yangdongi

cloth
걸레
geolle

clothes horse
빨래 건조대
ppallae geonjodae

clothes pegs
빨래집게
ppallaejipge

dustpan
쓰레받기
sseurebatgi

iron
다리미
darimi

ironing board
다리미판
darimipan

mop
대걸레
daegeolle

rubber gloves
고무장갑
gomujanggap

scourer
수세미
susemi

tumble drier
빨래건조기
ppallaegeonjogi

vacuum cleaner
진공청소기
jingongcheongsogi

washing line
빨랫줄
ppallaetjul

washing machine
세탁기
setakgi

washing powder
분말 세제
bunmal seje

wastepaper basket
휴지통
hyujitong

AT THE SHOPS | 상점

You will not only find large supermarkets and shopping malls in Korean towns and cities, you will also come across convenience stores and small individual shops on every street corner. Some food markets and flea markets are popular amongst young people, especially those who want to enjoy shopping and street food at the same time.

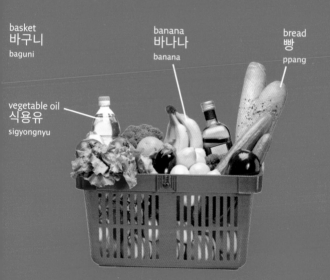

basket
바구니
baguni

banana
바나나
banana

bread
빵
ppang

vegetable oil
식용유
sigyongnyu

Many shops in Korea open later than in the UK – generally at 10 a.m. – but are then open until 8 p.m. or later, while convenience stores are open 24 hours a day. Large supermarket chains may close the second and fourth Sunday of every month, whereas the department stores and big shopping centres usually close once a month (usually on a Monday).

YOU MIGHT SAY...

Where is the nearest...?
가장 가까운 ... 이/가
어디에 있어요?
gajang gakkaun ... i/ga eodie isseoyo

Where can I buy...?
... 을/를 어디에서 살 수
있어요?
... eul/reul eodieseo sal su isseoyo

What time do you open/close?
몇 시에 문 열어요/닫아요?
myeot sie mun yeoreoyo/dadayo

I'm just looking.
그냥 구경 중이에요.
geunyang gugyeong jungieyo

Do you sell...?
... 팔아요?
... parayo

Can I pay by cash/card?
현금으로/카드로 계산해도
돼요?
hyeongeumeuro/kadeuro gyesanhaedo dwaeyo

Can I pay with my mobile app?
폰 앱으로 계산해도 돼요?
pon aebeuro gyesanhaedo dwaeyo

How much does this cost?
얼마예요?
eolmayeyo

How much is delivery?
배달은 얼마예요?
baedareun eolmayeyo

I need/would like...
... 을/를 사고 싶은데요.
... eul/reul sago sipeundeyo

Can I exchange this?
이거 교환 돼요?
igeo gyohwan dwaeyo

Can I get a refund?
이거 환불 돼요?
igeo hwanbul dwaeyo

Can you recommend...?
... 추천해 주실 수 있어요?
... chucheonhae jusil su isseoyo

That's all, thank you.
그게 다예요. 감사합니다.
geuge dayeyo. gamsahamnida

YOU MIGHT HEAR...

Can I help you?
무엇을 도와드릴까요?
mueoseul dowadeurilkkayo

Are you looking for anything in particular?
특별히 찾는 거 있으세요?
teukbyeolhi channeun geo isseuseyo

I would recommend...
... 을/를 추천드려요.
... eul/reul chucheondeuryeoyo

Would you like anything else?
다른 필요한 거 있으세요?
dareun piryohan geo isseuseyo

It costs...
... 원이에요.
... wonieyo

I'm sorry, we don't have...
죄송합니다, ... 은/는 없어요.
joesonghamnida, ... eun/neun eopseoyo

I can order that for you.
주문 가능합니다.
jumun ganeunghamnida

How would you like to pay?
어떻게 계산하시겠어요?
eotteoke gyesanhasigesseoyo

Can you enter your PIN?
비밀번호를 입력해 주세요.
bimilbeonhoreul imnyeokae juseyo

Would you like a receipt?
영수증 드릴까요?
yeongsujeung deurilkkayo

Have you got a receipt?
영수증 받으셨어요?
yeongsujeung badeusyeosseoyo

We'd love to see you again soon.
또 뵙겠습니다.
tto boepgetseumnida

VOCABULARY

shop
상점
sangjeom

supermarket
슈퍼마켓
syupeomaket

corner shop
구멍가게
gumeonggage

shopping centre
쇼핑센터
syopingsenteo

market
시장
sijang

cash
현금
hyeongeum

change
잔돈
jandon

PIN
비밀번호
bimilbeonho

checkout
계산대
gyesandae

exchange 교환 gyohwan	voucher 쿠폰 kupon	to buy 사다 sada
refund 환불 hwanbul	gift voucher 상품권 sangpumgwon	to pay 계산하다 gyesanhada
receipt 영수증 yeongsujeung	to browse 구경하다 gugyeonghada	to shop (online) (온라인에서) 사다 (ollaineseo) sada

banknotes
지폐
jipye

bin bag
쓰레기봉투
sseuregibongtu

card reader
카드 단말기
kadeu danmalgi

coins
동전
dongjeon

debit/credit card
직불/신용 카드
jikbul/sinyong kadeu

paper bag
종이봉투
jongibongtu

As in the UK, supermarkets in Korea offer online shopping and delivery services.

YOU MIGHT SAY...

Where can I find...?
... 어디에 있어요?
... eodie isseoyo

I'm looking for...
... 찾고 있어요.
... chatgo isseoyo

Do you have...?
... 있어요?
... isseoyo

YOU MIGHT HEAR...

We have/don't have...
... 있어요/없어요.
... isseoyo/eopseoyo

I can show you.
보여 드릴게요.
boyeo deurilgeyo

It's in aisle 1/2/3.
1번/2번/3번 통로에
있어요.
ilbeon/ibeon/sambeon tongnoe isseoyo

VOCABULARY

delivery service
배달 서비스
baedal seobiseu

shop assistant
상점 직원
sangjeom jigwon

aisle
통로
tongno

groceries
식료품
singnyopum

delicatessen
수입식품점
suipsikpumjeom

ready meal
즉석식품
jeukseoksikpum

bottle/jar
병
byeong

box
상자
sangja

carton
골판지 상자
golpanji sangja

multipack
멀티팩
meoltipaek

packet
묶음
mukkeum

tin
통
tong

fresh
신선한
sinseonhan

tinned
통조림
tongjorim

low-fat
저지방
jeojibang

frozen
냉동
naengdong

dairy
유제품
yujepum

low-calorie
저칼로리
jeokallori

GENERAL

basket
바구니
baguni

scales
저울
jeoul

trolley
쇼핑카트
syopingkateu

GROCERIES

biscuits
과자
gwaja

honey
꿀
kkul

instant coffee
인스턴트 커피
inseuteonteu keopi

jam
잼
jaem

ketchup
케첩
kecheop

noodles
면
myeon

olive oil
올리브 오일
ollibeu oil

pepper
후추
huchu

red chilli paste
고추장
gochujang

rice
쌀
ssal

salt
소금
sogeum

sesame oil
참기름
chamgireum

soybean paste
된장
doenjang

soy sauce
간장
ganjang

sugar
설탕
seoltang

teabags
티백
tibaek

vegetable oil
식용유
sigyongnyu

vinegar
식초
sikcho

SNACKS

chocolate
초콜릿
chokollit

crisps
감자칩
gamjachip

nuts
견과류
gyeongwaryu

popcorn
팝콘
papkon

rice cake
떡
tteok

sweets
단것
dangeot

DRINKS

beer
맥주
maekju

fizzy drink
탄산음료
tansaneumyo

fruit juice
과일주스
gwailjuseu

spirits
증류주
jeungnyuju

still water
물
mul

wine
와인
wain

MARKET | 시장

In Korean cities you can find several traditional markets which sell fresh fruit, vegetables, meat, fish, and street food. While many people in cities do their grocery shop in supermarkets, these traditional markets are popular with young people as well as foreigners as they provide a unique experience. You will also find antiques markets and flea markets in small alleys or parks. Some markets are open most days, others weekly or monthly.

YOU MIGHT SAY...

Do you have...?
... 있어요?
... isseoyo

Where is the market?
시장이 어디에 있어요?
sijangi eodie isseoyo

500 grams/A kilo of...
... 오백 그램/일 킬로
... obaek geuraem/il killo

Two/Three ..., please.
... 두 개/세 개 주세요.
... du gae/se gae juseyo

A slice of ..., please.
... 한 조각 주세요.
... han jogak juseyo

What do I owe you?
얼마예요?
eolmayeyo

YOU MIGHT HEAR...

The market is in the square.
시장은 광장에 있어요.
sijangeun gwangjange isseoyo

What would you like?
뭐 드릴까요?
mwo deurilkkayo

That will be...
... 원이에요.
... wonieyo

There is no more...
... 은/는 없어요.
... eun/neun eopseoyo

Anything else?
다른 필요한 거 있으세요?
dareun piryohan geo isseuseyo

Here's your change.
여기 잔돈이요.
yeogi jandoniyo

YOU SHOULD KNOW...

Night markets are popular in spring and autumn because the weather is mild and people take part in outside activities, even at night. You can find numerous stalls selling all sort of meals and snacks, as well as hand-made accessories.

indoor market 실내에 있는 시장 sillaee inneun sijang	night market 야시장 yasijang	seasonal 제철 jecheol
antiques market 골동품 시장 goldongpum sijang	local 지역 jiyeok	home-made 자체 제작한 jache jejakan
flea market 벼룩 시장 byeoruk sijang	organic 유기농 yuginong	hand-made 수제품 sujepum

MARKETPLACE

trader
상인
sangin

stall
노점
nojeom

plastic bag
비닐봉투
binilbongtu

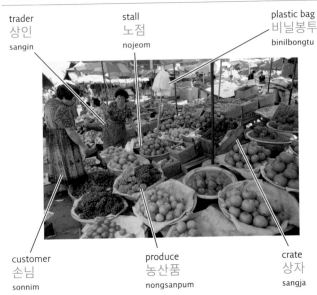

customer
손님
sonnim

produce
농산품
nongsanpum

crate
상자
sangja

Korean supermarkets offer a wide range of fruit and vegetables. When buying fruit or vegetables from the supermarket, customers are usually required to weigh and sticker their purchases before going to the checkout.

YOU MIGHT SAY...

Where can I buy...?
... 어디에서 사요?
... eodieseo sayo

Are they ripe/fresh?
잘 익었어요/신선해요?
jal igeosseoyo/sinseonhaeyo

YOU MIGHT HEAR...

What would you like?
뭐 드릴까요?
mwo deurilkkayo

They are ripe/very fresh.
익었어요/아주 신선해요.
igeosseoyo/aju sinseonhaeyo

VOCABULARY

grocer's 식료품점 singnyopumjeom	pip/seed/stone 씨 ssi	rotten 썩은 sseogeun
root vegetable 뿌리 야채 ppuri yachae	segment 한 쪽 han jjok	ripe 익은 igeun
juice 주스 juseu	core 속 sok	unripe 덜 익은 deol igeun
leaf 잎 ip	raw 날것 nalgeot	seedless 씨 없는 ssi eomneun
peel/rind/skin 껍질 kkeopjil	fresh 신선한 sinseonhan	to chop 썰다 sseolda

to dice
깍둑썰기를 하다
kkakdukseolgireul hada

to juice
즙을 내다
jeubeul naeda

to wash
씻다
ssitda

to grate
갈다
galda

to peel
껍질을 벗기다
kkeopjireul beotgida

YOU SHOULD KNOW...

Although Korea uses the metric system in general, there is a special unit called "근 (geun)", which is the most commonly used measurement of weight for meat (600g) or fruit and vegetables (375g).

FRUIT

apple
사과
sagwa

apricot
살구
salgu

banana
바나나
banana

blueberry
블루베리
beulluberi

cantaloupe
멜론
mellon

cherry
체리
cheri

grape
포도
podo

grapefruit
자몽
jamong

jujube
대추
daechu

kiwi fruit
키위
kiwi

Korean melon
참외
chamoe

lemon
레몬
remon

lychee
리치
richi

mango
망고
manggo

mulberry
오디
odi

orange
오렌지
orenji

peach
복숭아
boksunga

persimmon
감
gam

pineapple
파인애플
painaepeul

plum
자두
jadu

pomegranate
석류
seongnyu

strawberry
딸기
ttalgi

tangerine
귤
gyul

watermelon
수박
subak

VEGETABLES

asparagus
아스파라거스
aseuparageoseu

aubergine
가지
gaji

bamboo shoots
죽순
juksun

broccoli
브로콜리
beurokolli

cabbage
양배추
yangbaechu

carrot
당근
danggeun

cauliflower
콜리플라워
kollipeullawo

celery
셀러리
selleori

chilli
고추
gochu

Chinese cabbage
배추
baechu

courgette
주키니호박
jukinihobak

cucumber
오이
oi

garlic
마늘
maneul

ginger
생강
saenggang

lettuce
양상추
yangsangchu

lotus root
연근
yeongeun

mooli
무
mu

mushroom
버섯
beoseot

onion
양파
yangpa

pak choi
청경채
cheonggyeongchae

perilla leaves
깻잎
kkaennip

potato
감자
gamja

red pepper
파프리카
papeurika

spinach
시금치
sigeumchi

spring onion
파
pa

tomato
토마토
tomato

sweet potato
고구마
goguma

Ask the fishmonger for tips on what is fresh, what has been frozen, and what is in season.

YOU MIGHT SAY...

How fresh is this fish?
신선한 생선이에요?
sinseonhan saengseonieyo

I'd like the scales removed, please.
비늘 제거해 주세요.
bineul jegeohae juseyo

Are there a lot of bones in this fish?
이 생선에 뼈가 많아요?
i saengseone ppyeoga manayo

YOU MIGHT HEAR...

This fish was caught in the river this morning.
오늘 아침에 강에서 잡은 생선이에요.
oneul achime gangeseo jabeun saengseonieyo

Would you like the scales/guts removed?
비늘/내장 제거해 드릴까요?
bineul/naejang jegeohae deurilkkayo

VOCABULARY

fishmonger
생선 장수
saengseon jangsu

shellfish
패류
paeryu

scales
비늘
bineul

bone
뼈
ppyeo

shell
껍데기
kkeopdegi

roe
생선알
saengseonal

freshwater
민물
minmul

saltwater
바닷물
badanmul

farmed
양식
yangsik

wild
자연산
jayeonsan

salted
소금에 절인
sogeume jeorin

smoked
훈제
hunje

anchovy
멸치
myeolchi

carp
잉어
ingeo

cod
대구
daegu

eel
장어
jangeo

mackerel
고등어
godeungeo

monkfish
아귀
agwi

pollack
명태
myeongtae

salmon
연어
yeoneo

sea bass
농어
nongeo

sea bream
도미
domi

trout
송어
songeo

tuna
참치
chamchi

abalone
전복
jeonbok

clam
조개
jogae

crab
게
ge

lobster
바닷가재
badatgajae

mussel
홍합
honghap

octopus
문어
muneo

oyster
굴
gul

prawn/shrimp
새우
saeu

scallop
가리비
garibi

sea cucumber
해삼
haesam

sea urchin
성게
seongge

squid
오징어
ojingeo

YOU MIGHT SAY...

A kilo of...
... 일 킬로
... il killo

Can you slice this for me, please?
잘라 주실 수 있어요?
jalla jusil su isseoyo

Can you remove the bone, please?
뼈 제거해 주실 수 있어요?
ppyeo jegeohae jusil su isseoyo

YOU MIGHT HEAR...

Certainly, sir/madam.
물론이죠, 손님.
mullonijyo, sonnim

How much/many would you like?
얼마나 드릴까요?
eolmana deurilkkayo

Is half a kilo enough?
오백 그램 드리면 될까요?
obaek geuraem deurimyeon doelkkayo

VOCABULARY

butcher
정육업자
jeongyugeopja

meat
고기
gogi

red/white meat
붉은/흰살 고기
bulgeun/huinsal gogi

cold meats
냉육
naengyuk

pork
돼지고기
dwaejigogi

beef
소고기
sogogi

lamb
양고기
yanggogi

offal
내장
naejang

poultry
가금류
gageumnyu

chicken
닭고기
dakgogi

duck
오리고기
origogi

raw
날것
nalgeot

cooked
요리 된
yori doen

organic
유기농
yuginong

free-range
방목한
bangmokan

bacon
베이컨
beikeon

beefburger
소고기 버거
sogogi beogeo

ham
햄
haem

mince
다진 고기
dajin gogi

Korean beef
한우
hanu

ribs
갈비
galbi

sausage
소시지
sosiji

smoked duck
훈제오리
hunjeori

steak
스테이크
seuteikeu

Although European-style bread is becoming more popular in Korea, a loaf of bread in general tends to be sweeter or have a filling in it. Sweet and savoury buns, such as red bean buns or vegetable buns, are also common.

YOU MIGHT SAY...

Where is the...?
... 어디에 있어요?
... eodie isseoyo

What time do you open/close?
몇 시에 열어요/닫아요?
myeot sie yeoreoyo/dadayo

Do you sell...?
... 팔아요?
... parayo

May I have...?
... 주실 수 있어요?
... jusil su isseoyo

YOU MIGHT HEAR...

Are you being served?
주문 하셨어요?
jumun hasyeosseoyo

Would you like anything else?
다른 필요한 거 있으세요?
dareun piryohan geo isseuseyo

It costs...
... 원이에요.
... wonieyo

I'm sorry, we don't have...
죄송합니다, ... 은/는 없어요.
joesonghamnida, ... eun/neun eopseoyo

VOCABULARY

baker 제빵사 jeppangsa	cake 케이크 keikeu	flour 밀가루 milgaru
bread 빵 ppang	vegetable bun 야채빵 yachaeppang	gluten-free 글루텐 불포함 geulluten bulpoham
loaf 빵 한 덩이 ppang han deongi	dough 반죽 banjuk	to bake 굽다 gupda

baguette
바게트
bageteu

bread rolls
롤빵
rolppang

croissant
크루아상
keuruasang

Danish pastry
파이
pai

doughnut
도넛
doneot

éclair
에클레어
ekeulleeo

fruit tart
과일 타르트
gwail tareuteu

macaroon
마카롱
makarong

pancakes
팬케이크
paenkeikeu

red bean bun
단팥빵
danpatppang

waffle
와플
wapeul

wholemeal bread
통밀빵
tongmilppang

UHT milk and fresh milk is widely available in the supermarkets in Korea. It is also possible to find different types of cheeses, but the range might be somewhat limited.

VOCABULARY

egg white/yolk
계란 흰자/노른자
gyeran hinja/noreunja

cheese
치즈
chijeu

pasteurized/
unpasteurized
저온살균/저온살균
되지 않은
jeoonsalgyun/
jeoonsalgyun doeji aneun

UHT milk
멸균우유
myeolgyunuyu

caged
새장에 갇힌
saejange gachin

fresh milk
생우유
saenguyu

free-range
자연방사
jayeonbangsa

dairy-free
유제품 불포함
yujepum bulpoham

butter
버터
beoteo

cream
크림
keurim

egg
계란
gyeran

milk
우유
uyu

soymilk
두유
duyu

yoghurt
요구르트
yogureuteu

Most medicines should be purchased in a pharmacy in Korea. Some basic medicines such as painkillers or cough mixture are available at supermarkets or convenience stores.

YOU MIGHT SAY...

I need something for...
... 약을 사고 싶은데요.
... yageul sago sipeundeyo

I'm allergic to...
... 에 알레르기가 있어요.
... e allereugiga isseoyo

What would you recommend?
추천해 주시겠어요?
chucheonhae jusigesseoyo

Is it suitable for young children?
애들이 먹어도 되나요?
aedeuri meogeodo doenayo

YOU MIGHT HEAR...

Do you have a prescription?
처방전 가지고 계세요?
cheobangjeon gajigo gyeseyo

Do you have any allergies?
혹시 알레르기가 있나요?
hoksi allereugiga innayo

Take two tablets twice a day.
하루에 두알 씩, 두 번
드세요.
harue dual ssik, du beon deuseyo

You should see a doctor.
병원에 가셔야 합니다.
byeongwone gasyeoya hamnida

You need a prescription to buy that.
처방전이 있어야 살 수
있어요.
cheobangjeoni isseoya sal su isseoyo

I'd recommend...
... 을/를 추천드려요.
... eul/reul chucheondeuryeoyo

VOCABULARY

pharmacist
약사
yaksa

counter
판매대
panmaedae

antihistamine
항알레르기약
hangallereugiyak

cabinet
약장
yakjang

prescription
처방전
cheobangjeon

antiseptic
소독약
sodongnyak

97

decongestant	diarrhoea tablets	hay fever
비충혈 제거제	지사제	꽃가루 알레르기
bichunghyeol jegeoje	jisaje	kkotgaru allereugi

medicine	tube	headache
약	튜브	두통
yak	tyubeu	dutong

ointment	cold	sore throat
연고	감기	인후염
yeongo	gamgi	inhuyeom

painkiller	flu	stomachache
진통제	독감	복통
jintongje	dokgam	boktong

flu tablets	diarrhoea	asthma
독감 약	설사	천식
dokgam yak	seolsa	cheonsik

YOU SHOULD KNOW...

Hygiene and beauty items are not available in pharmacies in Korea, but are sold in a beauty shop.

GENERAL

antiseptic cream
소독용 크림
sodogyong keurim

bandage
붕대
bungdae

capsule
캡슐
kaepsyul

condom
콘돔
kondom

cough mixture
기침약
gichimnyak

drops
물약
mullyak

insect repellent
방충제
bangchungje

lozenge
목캔디
mokkaendi

plaster
반창고
banchanggo

protective face mask
마스크
maseukeu

sun cream
선크림
seonkeurim

tablet/pill
알약
allyak

HYGIENE

antiperspirant
땀 억제제
ttam eokjeje

conditioner
린스
rinseu

mouthwash
구강 세정제
gugang sejeongje

razor
면도칼
myeondokal

sanitary towel
생리대
saengnidae

shampoo
샴푸
syampu

shaving foam
쉐이빙폼
sweibingpom

shower gel
샤워 젤
syawo jel

soap
비누
binu

tampon
탐폰
tampon

toothbrush
칫솔
chitsol

toothpaste
치약
chiyak

blusher
블러셔
beulleosyeo

comb
꼬리빗
kkoribit

eyeliner
아이라이너
airaineo

eyeshadow
아이섀도
aisyaedo

foundation
파운데이션
paundeisyeon

hairbrush
빗
bit

hairspray
헤어스프레이
heeoseupeurei

lip balm
립밤
ripbam

lipstick
립스틱
ripseutik

mascara
마스카라
maseukara

nail varnish
매니큐어
maenikyueo

powder
파우더
paudeo

VOCABULARY

dummy 공갈젖꼭지 gonggaljeotkkokji	to be teething 젖니가 나다 jeonniga nada	to breast-feed 모유 수유하다 moyu suyuhada

CLOTHING

Babygro®/sleepsuit
아기우주복
agiujubok

baby shoes
아기신발
agisinbal

bib
턱받이
teokbaji

mittens
벙어리장갑
beongeorijanggap

snowsuit
겨울우주복
gyeourujubok

vest
바디슈트
badisyuteu

HEALTH AND HYGIENE

baby food
유아식
yuasik

baby's bottle
젖병
jeotbyeong

changing bag
기저귀 가방
gijeogwi gabang

cotton bud
면봉
myeonbong

cotton wool
솜
som

formula milk
분유
bunyu

nappy
기저귀
gijeogwi

nappy cream
기저귀 크림
gijeogwi keurim

wet wipes
물티슈
multisyu

ACCESSORIES

baby bath
아기 욕조
agi yokjo

baby sling
포대기
podaegi

cot
아기 침대
agi chimdae

highchair
아기 의자
agi uija

pram
유모차
yumocha

pushchair
유모차
yumocha

Newsagents in Korea sell magazines, newspapers, and small snacks. Corner shops and convenience stores sell beverages, snacks, and cigarettes. Some stationery, like stamps and envelopes, can also be bought in a post office.

VOCABULARY

broadsheet 종합신문 jonghapsinmun	stationery 문구류 munguryu	vendor 노점상 nojeomsang
tabloid 타블로이드 tabeulloideu	snack 간식거리 gansikgeori	daily 일간지 ilganji
kiosk 무인 단말기 muin danmalgi	tobacconist 담배 가게 dambae gage	weekly 주간지 juganji

book
책
chaek

cigarette
담배
dambae

comic book
만화책
manhwachaek

confectionery
과자류
gwajaryu

envelope
봉투
bongtu

greetings card
인사 카드
insa kadeu

magazine
잡지
japji

map
지도
jido

newspaper
신문
sinmun

notebook
공책
gongchaek

pen
펜
pen

pencil
연필
yeonpil

scratch card
즉석복권
jeukseokbokgwon

postcard
엽서
yeopseo

stamp
우표
upyo

YOU MIGHT SAY...

Where is...?
... 어디에 있어요?
... eodie isseoyo

Which floor is this?
여기가 몇 층이에요?
yeogiga myeot cheungieyo

Can you gift-wrap this, please?
선물 포장해 주시겠어요?
seonmul pojanghae jusigesseoyo

YOU MIGHT HEAR...

Menswear is on the second floor.
남성복은 3층이에요.
namseongbogeun samcheungieyo

This is the first floor.
여기는 2층이에요.
yeogineun icheungieyo

Would you like this gift-wrapped?
선물 포장해 드릴까요?
seonmul pojanghae deurilkkayo

VOCABULARY

floor
층
cheung

counter
계산대
gyesandae

sportswear
운동복
undongbok

escalator
에스컬레이터
eseukeolleiteo

department
매장
maejang

swimwear
수영복
suyeongbok

lift
엘리베이터
ellibeiteo

menswear
남성복
namseongbok

brand
상표
sangpyo

toilets
화장실
hwajangsil

womenswear
여성복
yeoseongbok

sale
세일/할인
seil/harin

YOU SHOULD KNOW...

Note that the ground floor in the UK is the first floor in Korea; the first floor in the UK is the second floor in Korea, and so on.

accessories
액세서리
aekseseori

cosmetics
화장품
hwajangpum

fashion
의류
uiryu

food and drink
식음료
sigeumnyo

footwear
신발
sinbal

furniture
가구
gagu

kitchenware
주방용품
jubangyongpum

leather goods
가죽 제품
gajuk jepum

lighting
조명
jomyeong

lingerie
여성 속옷
yeoseong sogot

soft furnishings
가정용 직물 제품
gajeongyong jingmul
jepum

toys
장난감
jangnangam

YOU MIGHT SAY...

I'm just looking.
그냥 구경 중이에요.
geunyang gugyeong jungieyo

I'd like to try this on, please.
이거 입어 보고 싶은데요.
igeo ibeo bogo sipeundeyo

Where are the fitting rooms?
탈의실이 어디에 있어요?
taruisiri eodie isseoyo

I'm a size...
제 사이즈는 ... 이에요/예요.
je saijeuneun ... ieyo/yeyo

Have you got a bigger/smaller size?
이것보다 큰/작은 사이즈 있어요?
igeotboda keun/jageun saijeu isseoyo

This is too small/big.
이건 너무 작아요/커요.
igeon neomu jagayo/keoyo

This is too tight/short/long.
이건 너무 조여요/짧아요/길어요.
igeon neomu joyeoyo/jjalbayo/gireoyo

This is torn.
이건 찢어졌어요.
igeon jjijeojyeosseoyo

YOU MIGHT HEAR...

Can I help you?
무엇을 도와드릴까요?
mueoseul dowadeurilkkayo

The fitting rooms are over there.
탈의실은 저쪽이에요.
taruisireun jeojjogieyo

What (dress) size are you?
(옷은) 몇 사이즈 입으세요?
(oseun) myeot saijeu ibeuseyo

What shoe size are you?
신발은 몇 사이즈 신으세요?
sinbareun myeot saijeu sineuseyo

I'm sorry, it's out of stock.
죄송해요. 그 제품은 재고가 없어요.
joesonghaeyo. geu jepumeun jaegoga eopseoyo

I'm sorry, we don't have that size/colour.
죄송해요. 그 사이즈는/색깔은 없어요.
joesonghaeyo. geu saijeuneun/saekkkareun eopseoyo

That suits you.
잘 어울리세요.
jal eoulliseyo

VOCABULARY

fitting room 탈의실 taruisil	perfume 향수 hyangsu	leather 가죽 gajuk
clothes/clothing 옷 ot	aftershave 남성용 스킨케어 namseongyong seukinkeeo	silk 실크 silkeu
shoes/footwear 신발 sinbal	jewellery 보석류 boseongnyu	size (clothing) 옷 사이즈 ot saijeu
underwear 속옷 sogot	wool 모직 mojik	size (shoe) 신발 사이즈 sinbal saijeu
wallet/purse 지갑 jigap	denim 데님 denim	to try on 입어 보다 ibeo boda
umbrella 우산 usan	cotton 면 myeon	to fit 딱 맞다 ttak matda

YOU SHOULD KNOW...

It can be quite difficult to find clothes bigger than UK size 16, or shoes bigger than UK size 10 in Korea.

CLOTHING

bikini
비키니
bikini

blouse
블라우스
beullauseu

coat
외투
oetu

dressing gown
실내용 가운
sillaeyong gaun

dungarees
멜빵 바지
melppang baji

jacket
재킷
jaekit

jeans
청바지
cheongbaji

jogging bottoms
트레이닝 바지
teureining baji

jumper
스웨터
seuweteo

leggings
레깅스
regingseu

pants
팬티
paenti

pyjamas
잠옷
jamot

shirt
셔츠
syeocheu

shorts
반바지
banbaji

skirt
치마
chima

socks
양말
yangmal

sweatshirt
운동복 상의
undongbok sangui

swimsuit
원피스 수영복
wonpiseu suyeongbok

(three-piece) suit
(스리피스) 정장
(seuripiseu) jeongjang

tie
넥타이
nektai

tights
스타킹
seutaking

trousers
바지
baji

T-shirt
티셔츠
tisyeocheu

waterproof jacket
방수 재킷
bangsu jaekit

ACCESSORIES

baseball cap
야구 모자
yagu moja

belt
벨트
belteu

bracelet
팔찌
paljji

earrings
귀걸이
gwigeori

gloves
장갑
janggap

handbag
핸드백
haendeubaek

necklace
목걸이
mokgeori

scarf
스카프
seukapeu

woolly hat
털모자
teolmoja

FOOTWEAR

court shoes
여성용 구두
yeoseongyong gudu

high heels
하이힐
haihil

lace-up shoes
끈 달린 신발
kkeun dallin sinbal

sandals
샌들
saendeul

slippers
슬리퍼
seullipeo

trainers
운동화
undonghwa

DIY is becoming more popular in Korea as rising house prices mean that many people buy old houses to renovate. However, it is also very affordable to have specialist tradespeople in to carry out home improvements.

VOCABULARY

home improvements
주택 개조
jutaek gaejo

painting
페인트칠
peinteuchil

power tool
전동 공구
jeondong gonggu

joinery
소목일
somogil

decorating
꾸미기
kkumigi

to do DIY
직접하다
jikjeopada

HOME

drill
드릴
deuril

hammer
망치
mangchi

nails
못
mot

nuts and bolts
너트와 볼트
neoteuwa bolteu

paint
페인트
peinteu

paintbrush
페인트 붓
peinteu but

pliers
펜치
penchi

saw
톱
top

screwdriver
드라이버
deuraibeo

screws
나사
nasa

spanner
스패너
seupaeneo

stepladder
접이식 사다리
jeobisik sadari

tiles
타일
tail

wallpaper
벽지
byeokji

wrench
렌치
renchi

GARDEN

garden fork
갈퀴
galkwi

gardening gloves
원예용 장갑
wonyeyong janggap

pruners
원예용 가위
wonyeyong gawi

spade
삽
sap

trowel
모종삽
mojongsap

watering can
물뿌리개
mulppurigae

antique shop
골동품 가게
goldongpum gage

barber's
이발소
ibalso

beauty salon
뷰티 살롱
byuti sallong

bookshop
서점
seojeom

car showroom
자동차 전시장
jadongcha jeonsijang

convenience store
편의점
pyeonuijeom

department store
백화점
baekwajeom

electrical retailer
전자 제품 가게
jeonja jepum gage

estate agency
부동산 중개소
budongsan junggaeso

florist's
꽃 가게
kkot gage

furniture store
가구점
gagujeom

garden centre
화원
hwawon

gift shop
선물 가게
seonmul gage

hairdresser's
미용실
miyongsil

hardware shop
철물점
cheolmuljeom

jeweller's shop
금은방
geumeunbang

music shop
악기점
akgijeom

optician's
안경점
angyeongjeom

pet shop
애완 동물 용품점
aewan dongmul yongpumjeom

phone shop
핸드폰 가게
haendeupon gage

shoe shop
신발 가게
sinbal gage

stationer's
문구점
mungujeom

tea shop
차 파는 가게
cha paneun gage

travel agent's
여행사
yeohaengsa

DAY-TO-DAY | 일상생활

Business meetings, meals with friends, or courses of study... whatever your day-to-day schedule looks like during your time in Korea, this section deals with the words and phrases you may require when going on errands, planning outings, and going about your everyday business.

coffee with milk
밀크커피
milkeukeopi

handle
손잡이
sonjabi

cup
잔
jan

saucer
잔 받침
jan batchim

YOU MIGHT SAY...

Where are you going?
어디에 가요?
eodie gayo

What time do you finish?
몇 시에 끝나요?
myeot sie kkeunnayo

What are you doing today/tonight?
오늘/오늘 밤에 뭐 해요?
oneul/oneul bame mwo haeyo

Are you free on Friday?
금요일에 시간 돼요?
geumyoire sigan dwaeyo

Where/When would you like to meet?
어디에서/언제 만날까요?
eodieseo/eonje mannalkkayo

YOU MIGHT HEAR...

I'm at work/uni.
일 해요/대학교에 다녀요.
il haeyo/daehakgyoe danyeoyo

I have a day off.
하루 쉬어요.
haru swieoyo

I'm going to/planning to...
... 려고 해요.
... ryeogo haeyo

Let's meet at 6 p.m./at the restaurant.
저녁 여섯시에/식당에서 만나요.
jeonyeok yeoseotsie/sikdangeseo mannayo

I can't meet up at 11 a.m., sorry.
오전 열한시는 안 돼요.
미안해요.
ojeon yeolhansineun an dwaeyo.
mianhaeyo

VOCABULARY

to wake up 일어나다 ireonada	to leave 떠나다 tteonada	to meet friends 친구를 만나다 chingureul mannada
to get dressed 옷을 입다 oseul ipda	to study 공부하다 gongbuhada	to go home 집에 가다 jibe gada
to arrive 도착하다 dochakada	to work 일하다 ilhada	to go to bed 잠자리에 들다 jamjarie deulda

Traditionally, people eat a lighter version of a main meal for breakfast which might include rice, soup, and small side dishes. However, some people prefer a Western-style breakfast. Commuters will sometimes buy a simple breakfast from convenience stores or coffee shops.

VOCABULARY

bread and butter 빵과 버터 ppanggwa beoteo	to spread 바르다 bareuda	to skip breakfast 아침식사를 거르다 achimsiksareul georeuda
bread and jam 빵과 잼 ppanggwa jaem	to have breakfast 아침식사를 하다 achimsiksareul hada	

cereal
시리얼
sirieol

chocolate spread
초코잼
chokojaem

coffee
커피
keopi

coffee with milk
밀크커피
milkeukeopi

green tea
녹차
nokcha

jam
잼
jaem

orange juice
오렌지 주스
orenji juseu

peanut butter
땅콩버터
ttangkongbeoteo

rice porridge
죽
juk

tea
차
cha

toast
토스트
toseuteu

yoghurt
요구르트
yogureuteu

side dish
반찬
banchan

rice
밥
bap

soup
국
guk

Korean meals often consist of several dishes served at the same time, rather than a meal with different courses. For dessert, people normally eat fruit or small snacks.

YOU MIGHT SAY...

What's for dinner?
저녁 뭐 먹어요?
jeonyeok mwo meogeoyo

What time is lunch?
몇 시에 점심 먹어요?
myeot sie jeomsim meogeoyo

Can I try it?
먹어봐도 돼요?
meogeobwado dwaeyo

YOU MIGHT HEAR...

We're having ... for dinner.
저녁에 ... 먹을 거예요.
jeonyeoge ... meogeul geoyeyo

Lunch is at midday.
점심은 정오에 먹어요.
jeomsimeun jeongoe meogeoyo

Dinner's ready!
저녁 준비 다 됐어요!
jeonyeok junbi da dwaesseoyo

VOCABULARY

lunch	dinner	to have lunch/dinner
점심식사	저녁식사	점심/저녁 식사를 하다
jeomsimsiksa	jeonyeoksiksa	jeomsim/jeonyeok siksareul hada

YOU SHOULD KNOW...

Korean people also enjoy the cuisine of other countries, such as Chinese, Japanese, and Western-style food.

STAPLE FOODS

noodle soup
국수
guksu

rice
밥
bap

rice cake soup
떡국
tteokguk

barbecued pork belly
삼겹살
samgyeopsal

braised beef ribs
갈비찜
galbijjim

braised chicken
찜닭
jjimdak

braised pork
보쌈
bossam

cold noodles
냉면
naengmyeon

dumplings
만두
mandu

fermented soybean
paste stew
된장찌개
doenjangjjigae

fried chicken with
spicy sauce
양념치킨
yangnyeomchikin

ginseng chicken soup
삼계탕
samgyetang

grilled beef
불고기
bulgogi

grilled fish
생선구이
saengseongui

kimchi
김치
kimchi

kimchi stew
김치찌개
gimchijjigae

marinated crab with
soy sauce
간장게장
ganjanggejang

pork cutlet
돈가스
dongaseu

rice with vegetables
and meat
비빔밥
bibimbap

savoury pancake
부침개
buchimgae

seafood soup
해물탕
haemultang

seasonal vegetables
나물
namul

seasoned raw beef
육회
yukoe

spicy stir-fried chicken
닭갈비
dakgalbi

spicy stir-fried octopus
낙지볶음
nakjibokkeum

steamed egg
계란찜
gyeranjjim

stir-fried glass noodles
잡채
japchae

DESSERTS

dried persimmon
곶감
gotgam

glutinous rice ball
doughnuts
찹쌀도넛
chapssaldoneot

honey cookie
약과
yakgwa

honey toast
허니브레드
heonibeuredeu

red bean shaved ice
dessert
팥빙수
patbingsu

rice cake
떡
tteok

sweet pancake
호떡
hotteok

sweet rice puff
강정
gangjeong

walnut ball cake
호두과자
hodugwaja

EATING OUT | 외식

Eating out is a very common social experience in Korean culture. Before you order, you will be brought water for the table and a moist towel for wiping your hands during the meal. After ordering, you will be offered complimentary kimchi and side dishes – you can ask for more if you want.

YOU MIGHT SAY...

I'd like to make a reservation.
예약하고 싶어요.
yeyakago sipeoyo

A table for four, please.
4명이에요.
nemyeongieyo

We're ready to order.
저희 주문할게요.
jeohi jumunhalgeyo

What would you recommend?
추천하는 요리가 있나요?
chucheonhaneun yoriga innayo

What are the specials today?
오늘 특별 요리가 뭐예요?
oneul teukbyeol yoriga mwoyeyo

I'd like...
저는 ... 주세요.
jeoneun ... juseyo

Can we have more side dishes, please?
반찬 더 먹을 수 있을까요?
banchan deo meogeul su isseulkkayo

Are there vegetarian/vegan options?
채식/비건 메뉴가 있어요?
chaesik/bigeon menyuga isseoyo

I'm allergic to...
... 에 알레르기가 있어요.
... e allereugiga isseoyo

Excuse me, this is cold.
실례지만, 이거 차가워요.
sillyejiman, igeo chagawoyo

This is not what I ordered.
이건 제가 주문한 음식이 아니에요.
igeon jega jumunhan eumsigi anieyo

That was delicious.
맛있었어요.
masisseosseoyo

We'd like to pay, please.
저희 계산할게요.
jeohi gyesanhalgeyo

YOU SHOULD KNOW...

In a restaurant, you may or may not be given your bill at your table. In general, people ask for the bill at the counter and pay on the way out.

YOU MIGHT HEAR...

At what time?
몇 시예요?
myeot siyeyo

How many people?
몇 분이세요?
myeot buniseyo

Sorry, we're fully booked.
죄송하지만, 예약이 다
찼어요.
joesonghajiman, yeyagi da chasseoyo

Would you like anything to drink?
음료는 어떤 걸로
하시겠어요?
eumnyoneun eotteon geollo
hasigesseoyo

Are you ready to order?
주문하시겠어요?
jumunhasigesseoyo

I would recommend...
... 을/를 추천드려요.
... eul/reul chucheondeuryeoyo

The specials today are...
오늘의 특별 요리는 ...
이에요/예요.
oneurui teukbyeol yorineun ... ieyo/
yeyo

Would you like more side dishes?
반찬 더 드릴까요?
banchan deo deurilkkayo

I will let the chef know.
주방장께 알려드릴게요.
jubangjangkke allyeodeurilgeyo

Enjoy your meal!
맛있게 드세요.
masitge deuseyo

VOCABULARY

set menu
세트 메뉴
seteu menyu

daily specials
오늘의 특별 요리
oneurui teukbyeol yori

service charge
서비스 요금
seobiseu yogeum

vegetarian
채식주의자
chaesikjuuija

vegan
비건
bigeon

gluten-free
글루텐 불포함
geulluten bulpoham

to order
주문하다
jumunhada

to pay the bill
계산하다
gyesanhada

to be served
서빙받다
seobingbatda

bar
바
ba

beer mug
맥주잔
maekjujan

bill
계산서
gyesanseo

chair
의자
uija

floor cushion
방석
bangseok

menu
메뉴판
menyupan

moist towel
물수건
mulsugeon

table
테이블
teibeul

tablecloth
테이블보
teibeulbo

table grill
불판
bulpan

tongs
집게
jipge

waiter/waitress
종업원
jongeobwon

chopsticks
젓가락
jeotgarak

glass
잔
jan

knife and fork
나이프와 포크
naipeuwa pokeu

plate
접시
jeopsi

rice bowl
밥그릇
bapgeureut

salt and pepper
소금과 후추
sogeumgwa huchu

serviette
냅킨
naepkin

soju glass
소주잔
sojujan

soup bowl
국그릇
gukgeureut

soy sauce and vinegar
간장과 식초
ganjanggwa sikcho

spoon
숟가락
sutgarak

toothpicks
이쑤시개
issusigae

FAST FOOD | 패스트푸드

There are different types of fast food available in Korea, from Western-style foods to traditional street food.

YOU MIGHT SAY...

I'd like to order, please.
주문해도 돼요?
jumunhaedo dwaeyo

Do you deliver?
배달 돼요?
baedal dwaeyo

I'm sitting in/taking away.
먹고 가요/포장이요.
meokgo gayo/pojangiyo

That's everything, thanks.
그게 다예요. 감사합니다.
geuge dayeyo. gamsahamnida

YOU MIGHT HEAR...

Can I help you?
무엇을 도와드릴까요?
mueoseul dowadeurilkkayo

Sit-in or takeaway?
드시고 가세요 아니면 포장이세요?
deusigo gaseyo animyeon pojangiseyo

We do/don't do delivery.
배달 돼요/안 돼요.
baedal dwaeyo/an dwaeyo

Would you like anything else?
또 필요한 거 있으세요?
tto piryohan geo isseuseyo

VOCABULARY

fast-food chain
패스트푸드 체인
paeseuteupudeu chein

food stall
노점
nojeom

street food
길거리 음식
gilgeori eumsik

vendor
노점상
nojeomsang

drive-thru
승차 구매
seungcha gumae

an order to go/
a takeaway
포장하다
pojanghada

delivery charge
배달비
baedalbi

to place an order
주문하다
jumunhada

to collect an order
주문을 찾아오다
jumuneul chajaoda

black pudding
순대
sundae

burger
버거
beogeo

cup noodle
컵라면
keomnamyeon

hot dog
핫도그
hatdogeu

Korean fish cake
어묵
eomuk

sandwich
샌드위치
saendeuwichi

seaweed rice roll
김밥
gimbap

set meal box
도시락
dosirak

spicy rice cakes
떡볶이
tteokbokki

steamed bun
호빵
hoppang

tornado potato
회오리 감자
hoeori gamja

triangle gimbap
삼각김밥
samgakgimbap

YOU MIGHT SAY/HEAR...

I'll give you a call later.
나중에 전화할게요.
najunge jeonhwahalgeyo

I'll email you.
메일 보낼게요.
meil bonaelgeyo

What's your number?
번호가 뭐예요?
beonhoga mwoyeyo

This is a bad line.
신호가 안 좋아요.
sinhoga an joayo

I don't have any signal.
신호가 안 잡혀요.
sinhoga an japyeoyo

May I have your email address?
이메일 주소를 알려
주시겠어요?
imeil jusoreul allyeo jusigesseoyo

The website address is...
웹 사이트 주소는 ... 이에요/
예요.
wep saiteu jusoneun ... ieyo/yeyo

What's the WiFi password?
와이파이 비밀번호가 뭐예요?
waipai bimilbeonhoga mwoyeyo

It's all one word.
다 한 글자예요.
da han geuljayeyo

It's upper/lower case.
대문자/소문자예요.
daemunja/somunjayeyo

VOCABULARY

post
우편
upyeon

social media
소셜 미디어
sosyeol midieo

email
이메일
imeil

email address
이메일 주소
imeil juso

internet
인터넷
inteonet

WiFi
와이파이
waipai

website
웹 사이트
wep saiteu

link
링크
ringkeu

icon
아이콘
aikon

app
앱
aep

data
데이터
deiteo

mobile phone
휴대폰
hyudaepon

landline
유선 전화
yuseon jeonhwa

phone call
전화
jeonhwa

text message
문자 메시지
munja mesiji

voice mail
음성 메시지
eumseong mesiji

touchscreen
터치스크린
teochiseukeurin

screen
화면
hwamyeon

button
버튼
beoteun

battery
배터리
baeteori

to make a phone call
전화하다
jeonhwahada

to send a text
문자를 보내다
munjareul bonaeda

to post (online)
(온라인에)
게시하다
(ollaine) gesihada

to download/upload
다운받다/
업로드하다
daunbatda/eomnodeuhada

to charge your phone
휴대폰을
충전하다
hyudaeponeul
chungjeonhada

to switch on/off
전원을 켜다/끄다
jeonwoneul kyeoda/
kkeuda

to click on
클릭하다
keullikada

GENERAL

cable
케이블
keibeul

charger
충전기
chungjeongi

computer
컴퓨터
keompyuteo

keyboard
키보드
kibodeu

mouse
마우스
mauseu

mouse mat
마우스 패드
mauseu paedeu

phone case
폰 케이스
pon keiseu

power pack
보조 배터리 팩
bojo baeteori paek

SIM card
심 카드
sim kadeu

smartphone
스마트폰
seumateupon

tablet
태블릿 피시
taebeullit pisi

wireless router
무선 공유기
museon gongyugi

In Korea, elementary school goes from age 6 to 12, middle school from age 12 to 15, and high school from age 15 to 18. This is followed by a four-year university degree or two years at college. Elementary school and middle school are compulsory. Nursery and kindergarten are optional, although most parents send their children to both.

YOU MIGHT SAY...

What are you studying?
뭐 공부해요?
mwo gongbuhaeyo

What year are you in?
몇 학년이에요?
myeot hangnyeonieyo

What's your favourite subject?
어떤 과목을 제일
좋아해요?
eotteon gwamogeul jeil joahaeyo

YOU MIGHT HEAR...

I'm studying...
... 을/를 공부해요.
... eul/reul gongbuhaeyo

I'm in the fourth grade at elementary school.
초등학교 4학년이에요.
chodeunghakgyo sahangnyeonieyo

I have an assignment.
과제가 있어요.
gwajega isseoyo

VOCABULARY

nursery school
어린이집
eorinijip

elementary school
초등학교
chodeunghakgyo

middle/high school
중/고등학교
jung/godeunghakgyo

college
전문대학
jeonmundaehak

university
대학교
daehakgyo

headteacher
교장 선생님
gyojang seonsaengnim

janitor
수위
suwi

timetable
시간표
siganpyo

lesson
수업
sueop

subject
과목
gwamok

lecture
강의
gangui

tutorial
과외
gwaoe

assignment	assembly hall	to learn
과제	강당	배우다
gwaje	gangdang	baeuda

homework	playing field	to teach
숙제	운동장	가르치다
sukje	undongjang	gareuchida

exam	playground	to revise
시험	놀이터	복습하다
siheom	noriteo	bokseupada

degree	halls of residence	to sit an exam
학위	기숙사	시험을 보다
hagwi	gisuksa	siheomeul boda

undergraduate	student union	to graduate
학부생	학생회	졸업하다
hakbusaeng	haksaenghoe	joreopada

postgraduate	student card	to study
대학원생	학생증	공부하다
daehagwonsaeng	haksaengjeung	gongbuhada

YOU SHOULD KNOW...

Most Korean schools have a school uniform policy. There are strict rules about wearing accessories.

SCHOOL

classroom
교실
gyosil

colouring pencils
색연필
saengnyeonpil

eraser
지우개
jiugae

exercise book
연습장
yeonseupjang

felt-tip pens
사인펜
sainpen

fountain pen
만년필
mannyeonpil

hole punch
펀치
peonchi

paper
종이
jongi

paper clip
클립
keullip

pen
볼펜
bolpen

pencil
연필
yeonpil

pencil case
필통
piltong

pupil
학생
haksaeng

ruler
자
ja

schoolbag
책가방
chaekgabang

scissors
가위
gawi

sharpener
연필깎이
yeonpilkkakki

stapler
호치키스
hochikiseu

teacher
선생님
seonsaengnim

textbook
교과서
gyogwaseo

whiteboard
화이트보드
hwaiteubodeu

HIGHER EDUCATION

campus
교정
gyojeong

canteen
학생 식당
haksaeng sikdang

lecture hall
강의실
ganguisil

lecturer
강사
gangsa

library
도서관
doseogwan

student
학생
haksaeng

THE OFFICE | 사무실

Office hours are usually from 9 a.m. to 6 p.m. and from Monday to Friday.
Many businesses will have a lunch break between 12 noon and 1 p.m.

YOU MIGHT SAY/HEAR...

Can we arrange a meeting?
회의를 할 수 있을까요?
hoeuireul hal su isseulkkayo

May I speak to...?
... 하고 통화할 수 있을까요?
... hago tonghwahal su isseulkkayo

Can you send me...?
... 을/를 보내주실 수
있어요?
... eul/reul bonaejusil su isseoyo

I have a meeting with...
... 하고 회의가 있어요.
... hago hoeuiga isseoyo

Mr/Ms ... is on the phone.
... 씨는 통화중이세요.
... ssineun tonghwajungiseyo

Here's my business card.
여기 제 명함입니다.
yeogi je myeonghamimnida

Who's calling?
어디신지 여쭤봐도 될까요?
eodisinji yeojjwobwado doelkkayo

Can I call you back?
제가 다시 전화드려도
될까요?
jega dasi jeonhwadeuryeodo doelkkayo

VOCABULARY

manager	client	figures
부장	고객	수치
bujang	gogaek	suchi

staff	business card	spreadsheet
직원	명함	스프레드시트
jigwon	myeongham	seupeuredeusiteu

colleague	human resources	presentation
동료	인사	발표
dongnyo	insa	balpyo

report
보고
bogo

ink cartridge
잉크 카트리지
ingkeu kateuriji

password
비밀번호
bimilbeonho

meeting
회의
hoeui

inbox
받은 메일함
badeun meilham

to give a presentation
발표를 하다
balpyoreul hada

conference call
전화 회의
jeonhwa hoeui

attachment
첨부 파일
cheombu pail

to hold a meeting
회의를 열다
hoeuireul yeolda

video conference
영상 회의
yeongsang hoeui

username
사용자명
sayongjamyeong

to log on/off
접속을 하다/끄다
jeopsogeul hada/kkeuda

GENERAL

desk
책상
chaeksang

filing cabinet
서류장
seoryujang

folder
파일
pail

in/out tray
서류함
seoryuham

laptop
노트북
noteubuk

notepad
수첩
sucheop

photocopier
복사기
boksagi

printer
인쇄기
inswaegi

ring binder
서류철
seoryucheol

scanner
스캐너
seukaeneo

sticky notes
포스트잇
poseuteuit

sticky tape
스카치테이프
seukachiteipeu

telephone
전화기
jeonhwagi

swivel chair
회전의자
hoejeonuija

USB stick
유에스비 스틱
yueseubi seutik

Most banks are open from 9 a.m. to 4 p.m. from Monday to Friday. ATMs charge commission if you withdraw money outside office hours.

YOU MIGHT SAY...

I'd like to...
... 고 싶어요.
... go sipeoyo

... register for online banking.
인터넷 뱅킹 등록
inteonet baengking deungnok

Is there a fee for this service?
이 서비스에 요금이
있어요?
i seobiseue yogeumi isseoyo

I need to cancel my debit/credit card.
직불/신용 카드를 취소하고
싶어요.
jikbul/sinyong kadeureul chwisohago sipeoyo

YOU MIGHT HEAR...

May I see your ID, please?
신분증 보여주시겠어요?
sinbunjeung boyeojusigesseoyo

How much would you like to withdraw/deposit?
얼마나 인출/입금
하시겠어요?
eolmana inchul/ipgeum hasigesseoyo

Could you enter your PIN, please?
비밀번호 입력해 주시겠어요?
bimilbeonho imnyeokae jusigesseoyo

You must fill out an application form.
양식을 작성해 주셔야 합니다.
yangsigeul jakseonghae jusyeoya hamnida

VOCABULARY

branch
지점
jijeom

bank account
은행 계좌
eunhaeng gyejwa

account number
계좌 번호
gyejwa beonho

cashier
출납원
chullabwon

current account
입출금 계좌
ipchulgeum gyejwa

bank balance
은행 잔고
eunhaeng jango

online banking
인터넷 뱅킹
inteonet baengking

savings account
예금 계좌
yegeum gyejwa

bank statement
입출금 내역서
ipchulgeum naeyeokseo

overdraft
당좌대월
dangjwadaewol

loan
대출
daechul

to withdraw funds
자금을 회수하다
jageumeul hoesuhada

bank transfer
계좌 이체
gyejwa iche

mortgage
주택 담보 대출
jutaek dambo daechul

to make a deposit
예금하다
yegeumhada

chequebook
수표장
supyojang

interest
이자
ija

to open an account
계좌를 개설하다
gyejwareul gaeseolhada

currency
통화
tonghwa

to borrow
빌리다
billida

to change money
환전하다
hwanjeonhada

ATM
현금 자동 입출금기
hyeongeum jadong ipchulgeumgi

banknotes
지폐
jipye

bureau de change
환전소
hwanjeonso

debit/credit card
직불/신용 카드
jikbul/sinyong kadeu

exchange rate
환율
hwanyul

safety deposit box
대여 금고
daeyeo geumgo

Opening hours for post offices vary widely from place to place. Be aware that most post offices will ask about the contents of a parcel.

YOU MIGHT SAY...

I'd like to send this by airmail.
항공으로 보내고 싶어요.
hanggongeuro bonaego sipeoyo

Can I have a certificate of postage, please?
발송 증명서를 받을 수 있을까요?
balsong jeungmyeongseoreul badeul su isseulkkayo

How long will delivery take?
배송은 얼마나 걸려요?
baesongeun eolmana geollyeoyo

I'd like 4 stamps, please.
우표 4장 주세요.
upyo nejang juseyo

YOU MIGHT HEAR...

Place it on the scales, please.
저울에 올려 주세요.
jeoure ollyeo juseyo

What are the contents?
내용물이 뭐예요?
naeyongmuri mwoyeyo

What is the value of this parcel?
소포 내용물 가격이 어떻게 돼요?
sopo naeyongmur gagyeogi eotteoke dwaeyo

Would you like a certificate of postage?
발송 증명서를 드릴까요?
balsong jeungmyeongseoreul deurilkkayo

VOCABULARY

address	courier	to post
주소	배달원	부치다
juso	baedarwon	buchida
postal van	mail	to send
우편 배달차	우편	보내다
upyeon baedalcha	upyeon	bonaeda

YOU SHOULD KNOW...

While post offices are still popular with the older generation in Korea, express delivery companies are taking over the market with the services they provide, which many Korean people find quicker and more convenient.

box
상자
sangja

bubble wrap
뽁뽁이
ppokppogi

envelope
봉투
bongtu

letter
편지
pyeonji

package
소포
sopo

postal worker
우체국 직원
ucheguk jigwon

postbox
우체통
uchetong

postcard
엽서
yeopseo

stamp
우표
upyo

YOU MIGHT SAY...

How do I get to the city centre?
시내에 어떻게 가요?
sinaee eotteoke gayo

I need to go to...
... 에 가야 해요.
... e gaya haeyo

I'd like to visit...
... 에 가고 싶어요.
... e gago sipeoyo

What are the opening hours?
영업 시간이 언제예요?
yeongeop sigani eonjeyeyo

YOU MIGHT HEAR...

It's open between ... and...
... 시에서 ... 시 사이에
열어요.
... sieseo ... si saie yeoreoyo

It's closed on Mondays.
월요일에는 문 닫아요.
woryoireneun mun dadayo

PLACES OF IMPORTANCE

café
카페
kape

church
교회
gyohoe

cinema
영화관
yeonghwagwan

conference centre
콘퍼런스 센터
konpeoreonseu senteo

courthouse
법원
beobwon

dry cleaner's
세탁소
setakso

fire station
소방서
sobangseo

fountain
분수
bunsu

hospital
병원
byeongwon

hotel
호텔
hotel

library
도서관
doseogwan

mosque
모스크
moseukeu

office block
사무실 건물
samusil geonmul

park
공원
gongwon

playground
놀이터
noriteo

police station
경찰서
gyeongchalseo

shopping centre
쇼핑몰
syopingmol

town hall
시청
sicheong

146

A day trip, a break away, a night out, maybe even a night in – we all like to spend our free time differently. It's also a common topic of conversation with friends and colleagues; who doesn't like talking about holidays, hobbies, and how they like to hang out?

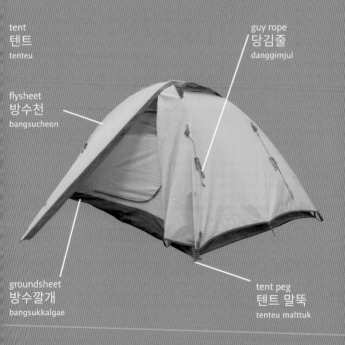

tent
텐트
tenteu

guy rope
당김줄
danggimjul

flysheet
방수천
bangsucheon

groundsheet
방수깔개
bangsukkalgae

tent peg
텐트 말뚝
tenteu malttuk

YOU MIGHT SAY...

What would you like to do?
뭐 하는 거 좋아해요?
mwo haneun geo joahaeyo

What do you do in your spare time?
여가시간에 뭐 해요?
yeogasigane mwo haeyo

Have you got any hobbies?
취미가 있어요?
chwimiga isseoyo

Are you sporty/creative/musical?
운동을/창의적인 것을/
음악을 좋아해요?
undongeul/changuijeogin geoseul/
eumageul joahaeyo

Do you enjoy...?
... 을/를 좋아해요?
... eul/reul joahaeyo

How did you get into...?
... 을/를 어떻게 시작하게
됐어요?
... eul/reul eotteoke sijakage dwaesseoyo

YOU MIGHT HEAR...

My hobbies include...
제 취미는 ... 이에요/예요.
je chwimineun ... ieyo/yeyo

I like...
... 좋아해요.
... joahaeyo

I really enjoy it.
정말 좋아해요.
jeongmal joahaeyo

It's not for me.
제 취향은 아니에요.
je chwihyangeun anieyo

I'm going on holiday.
휴가 가요.
hyuga gayo

I have/don't have a lot of spare time.
여가시간이 많아요/많이
없어요.
yeogasigani manayo/mani eopseoyo

VOCABULARY

activity 활동 hwaldong	to be interested in... ... 에 관심이 있다 ... e gwansimi itda	to relax 쉬다 swida
hobby/pastime 취미 chwimi	to pass the time 시간을 보내다 siganeul bonaeda	to enjoy 즐기다 jeulgida

148

cooking
요리
yori

DIY
직접 수리·조립하기
jikjeop suri·joripagi

gaming
게임
geim

going to karaoke
노래방 가기
noraebang gagi

jogging
조깅
joging

listening to music
음악 듣기
eumak deutgi

reading
독서
dokseo

shopping
쇼핑
syoping

sports
운동
undong

travelling
여행
yeohaeng

walking
걷기
geotgi

watching TV/films
티브이/영화 보기
tibeui/yeonghwa bogi

SIGHTSEEING | 관광

Korea has around 10 million visitors every year. The country offers travellers a range of experiences from buzzing modern cities to timeless traditions and beautiful landscapes.

YOU MIGHT SAY...

How much is it to get in?
입장하는 데 얼마예요?
ipjanghaneun de eolmayeyo

Is there a discount for...?
... 할인이 있어요?
... harini isseoyo

Where is the tourist office?
관광 안내소가 어디에
있어요?
gwangwang annaesoga eodie isseoyo

Are there sightseeing tours?
관광 안내 투어가 있어요?
gwangwang annae tueoga isseoyo

YOU MIGHT HEAR...

Entry costs...
입장료는 ... 원이에요.
ipjangnyoneun ... wonieyo

The tourist office is located...
관광 안내소는 ... 에 있어요.
gwangwang annaesoneun ... e isseoyo

There is a guided tour you can book.
가이드 투어를 예약할 수
있어요.
gaideu tueoreul yeyakal su isseoyo

Audio guides are/are not available.
오디오 가이드가 있어요/
없어요.
odio gaideuga isseoyo/eopseoyo

VOCABULARY

tourist	excursion	audio guide
관광객	여행	오디오 가이드
gwangwanggaek	yeohaeng	odio gaideu
tourist attraction	historic site	to visit
관광지	유적지	방문하다
gwangwangji	yujeokji	bangmunhada

YOU SHOULD KNOW...

Bear in mind that some cultural and historical sites, such as museums and art galleries, are closed on certain days of the week (usually Monday). Some religious sites may also require visitors to observe a certain dress code.

art gallery
미술관
misulgwan

camera
사진기
sajingi

city map
관광 지도
gwangwang jido

gardens
정원
jeongwon

guidebook
관광 안내서
gwangwang annaeseo

monument
기념비
ginyeombi

museum
박물관
bangmulgwan

palace
궁
gung

sightseeing bus
관광버스
gwangwangbeoseu

temple
절
jeol

tour guide
관광 안내원
gwangwang annaewon

tourist office
관광 안내소
gwangwang annaeso

When it comes to nightlife in Korea's towns and cities, check the tourist office for information on local events and venues. Why not get recommendations on bars and clubs from residents too?

YOU MIGHT SAY...

What is there to do at night?
밤에 할 수 있는게 뭐 있어요?
bame hal su inneunge mwo isseoyo

What's on at the cinema/theatre?
지금 영화관에서/극장에서
뭐 해요?
jigeum yeonghwagwaneseo/
geukjangeseo mwo haeyo

Where are the best bars/clubs?
제일 좋은 바나 클럽이
어디예요?
jeil joeun bana keulleobi eodiyeyo

Do you want to go and see a...?
... 보러 갈래요?
... boreo gallaeyo

Are there tickets for...?
... 표 있어요?
... pyo isseoyo

Two seats in the stalls, please.
1층에 자리 두 개 주세요.
ilcheunge jari dugae juseyo

What time does it start?
몇 시에 시작해요?
myeot sie sijakaeyo

YOU MIGHT HEAR...

The nightlife is great around here.
여기 밤에 할 게 많아요.
yeogi bame hal ge manayo

My favourite bar/club is...
제가 가장 좋아하는 바는/
클럽은...
jega gajang joahaneun baneun/
keulleobeun...

There's a film/show I'd like to see.
보고 싶은 영화가/공연이
있어요.
bogo sipeun yeonghwaga/gongyeoni
isseoyo

There are no tickets left.
표가 없어요.
pyoga eopseoyo

It begins at 7 o'clock.
7시에 시작해요.
ilgopsie sijakaeyo

Please turn off your mobile phones.
휴대폰을 꺼 주세요.
hyudaeponeul kkeo juseyo

VOCABULARY

nightlife
밤문화
bammunhwa

party
파티
pati

show
공연
gongyeon

film
영화
yeonghwa

play
연극
yeongeuk

festival
축제
chukje

box office
매표소
maepyoso

to socialize
사람들과 어울리다
saramdeulgwa eoullida

to go out
외출하다
oechulhada

to order food/drinks
음식을/음료를
주문하다
eumsigeul/eumnyoreul
jumunhada

to see a show
공연을 보다
gongyeoneul boda

to watch a film
영화를 보다
yeonghwareul boda

to go dancing
춤추러 가다
chumchureo gada

to enjoy oneself
즐거운 시간을
보내다
jeulgeoun siganeul
bonaeda

YOU SHOULD KNOW...

In order to experience Korea's diverse culture, traditional performances are something that you don't want to miss. There are various music and dance events, such as a narrative performance called 판소리 (pansori), a percussion performance by farmers known as 풍물놀이 (pungmullori), and 부채춤 (buchaechum), a dance with fans. You can even watch a performance in taekwondo!

ballet
발레
balle

bar
바
ba

busking
길거리 공연
gilgeori gongyeon

casino
카지노
kajino

cinema
영화관
yeonghwagwan

concert
콘서트
konseoteu

crosstalk
만담
mandam

funfair
이동 유원지
idong yuwonji

karaoke
노래방
noraebang

musical
뮤지컬
myujikeol

nightclub
나이트클럽
naiteukeulleop

opera
오페라
opera

restaurant
식당
sikdang

theatre
극장
geukjang

traditional performance
전통 공연
jeontong gongyeon

Korea offers a wide choice of places to stay from hostels or guest houses to luxurious hotels. Staying in a temple, known as a "templestay" 템플스테이 (tempeulseutei), or in a traditional house is also a popular option for those who want to have a unique and special experience.

YOU MIGHT SAY...

I have a reservation.
예약을 했어요.
yeyageul haesseoyo

What time is breakfast served?
조식은 몇 시예요?
josigeun myeot siyeyo

Have you got rooms available?
방이 있어요?
bangi isseoyo

What time do I have to check out?
체크아웃 시간은 언제예요?
chekeuaut siganeun eonjeyeyo

How much is it per night?
하룻밤에 얼마예요?
harutbame eolmayeyo

Could I upgrade my room?
제 방을 업그레이드 할 수 있을까요?
je bangeul eopgeureideu hal su isseulkkayo

I'd like to book a single/double room, please.
싱글 룸/더블 룸 예약하려고요.
singgeul rum/deobeul rum yeyakaryeogoyo

I need fresh towels for my room.
새 수건을 받고 싶어요.
sae sugeoneul batgo sipeoyo

Is breakfast included?
조식이 포함되어 있어요?
josigi pohamdoeeo isseoyo

I've lost my key.
열쇠를 잃어버렸어요.
yeolsoereul ireobeoryeosseoyo

I'd like to check in/out, please.
체크인/체크아웃 하려고요.
chekeuin/chekeuaut haryeogoyo

I'd like to make a complaint.
불만사항이 있어요.
bulmansahangi isseoyo

YOU SHOULD KNOW...

When checking in at your hotel, you may be expected to fill out a registration form and provide your passport number.

We have/don't have rooms available.
방이 있어요/없어요.
bangi isseoyo/eopseoyo

May I have your room number, please?
몇 호에 계시죠?
myeot hoe gyesijyo

Our rates are...
방 요금은 ... 원이에요.
bang yogeumeun ... wonieyo

May I see your documents, please?
서류를 볼 수 있을까요?
seoryureul bol su isseulkkayo

Breakfast is/is not included.
조식 포함이에요/
불포함이에요.
josik pohamieyo/bulpohamieyo

You may check in after...
체크인은 ... 시 이후에
가능해요.
chekeuineun ... si ihue ganeunghaeyo

Breakfast is served at...
조식은 ... 시에 드실 수
있어요.
josigeun ... sie deusil su isseoyo

You must check out before...
... 시까지 체크아웃 하셔야
해요.
... sikkaji chekeuaut hasyeoya haeyo

VOCABULARY

inn
여관
yeogwan

half board
두 끼 식사 제공
du kki siksa jegong

per person per night
일인당 하룻밤에
irindang harutbame

bed and breakfast
민박
minbak

room service
룸서비스
rumseobiseu

to check in
체크인하다
chekeuinhada

room only
식사 불포함
siksa bulpoham

wake-up call
모닝콜
moningkol

to check out
체크아웃하다
chekeuautada

full board
세 끼 식사 제공
se kki siksa jegong

room number
방 번호
bang beonho

to order room service
룸서비스를
주문하다
rumseobiseureul
jumunhada

corridor
복도
bokdo

"do not disturb" sign
"방해하지 마시오"
표시
"banghaehaji masio" pyosi

double room
더블 룸
deobeul rum

key card
카드식 열쇠
kadeusik yeolsoe

minibar
미니바
miniba

porter
포터
poteo

reception
프런트
peureonteu

receptionist
호텔 직원
hotel jigwon

safe
금고
geumgo

single room
싱글 룸
singgeul rum

toiletries
세면도구
semyeondogu

twin room
트윈 룸
teuwin rum

Camping is gaining in popularity in Korea. There are more and more camping sites popping up around the country; you can check online for reviews and recommendations.

YOU MIGHT SAY...

Have you got spaces available?
자리가 있어요?
jariga isseoyo

I'd like to book for ... nights.
... 박 예약하려고요.
... bak yeyakaryeogoyo

How much is it per night?
하룻밤에 얼마예요?
harutbame eolmayeyo

Where is the toilet/shower block?
화장실이/샤워장이 어디에 있어요?
hwajangsiri/syawojangi eodie isseoyo

Is the water drinkable?
그 물 마셔도 돼요?
geu mul masyeodo dwaeyo

YOU MIGHT HEAR...

We have spaces available.
자리가 있어요.
jariga isseoyo

We don't have spaces available.
자리가 없어요.
jariga eopseoyo

It costs ... per night.
하룻밤에 ... 원이에요.
harutbame ... wonieyo

The toilets/showers are located...
화장실은/샤워장은 ... 에 있어요.
hwajangsireun/syawojangeun ... e isseoyo

The water is/is not drinkable.
그 물 마셔도 돼요/못 마셔요.
geu mul masyeodo dwaeyo/mot masyeoyo

VOCABULARY

camper
캠핑하는 사람
kaempinghaneun saram

pitch
캠핑 자리
kaemping jari

toilet/shower block
화장실/샤워장
hwajangsil/syawojang

campsite
캠핑장
kaempingjang

electricity hook-up
캠핑용 멀티탭
kaempingyong meoltitaep

groundsheet
방수깔개
bangsukkalgae

to camp
캠핑하다
kaempinghada

to pitch a tent
텐트를 치다
tenteureul chida

to take down a tent
텐트를 걷다
tenteureul geotda

YOU SHOULD KNOW...

If you plan on holidaying with a caravan in Korea, remember that you will need a driving licence which is valid for the weight of the caravan.

air bed
에어 매트
eeo maeteu

camping stove
버너
beoneo

caravan
캠핑 트레일러
kaemping teureilleo

cool box
아이스박스
aiseubakseu

matches
성냥
seongnyang

motorhome
캠핑카
kaempingka

sleeping bag
침낭
chimnang

tent
텐트
tenteu

torch
손전등
sonjeondeung

Korea has a wonderful coastline with numerous islands and many beautiful beaches. Seaside activities are popular from mid June to late August.

YOU MIGHT SAY...

Is there a good beach nearby?
괜찮은 해변이 근처에 있어요?
gwaenchaneun haebyeoni geuncheoe isseoyo

Is swimming permitted here?
여기에서 수영해도 돼요?
yeogieseo suyeonghaedo dwaeyo

Is the water cold?
물이 차가워요?
muri chagawoyo

Can we hire...?
... 빌릴 수 있어요?
... billil su isseoyo

Help!
도와주세요!
dowajuseyo

YOU MIGHT HEAR...

This is a public beach.
여기가 해수욕장이에요.
yeogiga haesuyokjangieyo

Swimming is allowed/forbidden.
수영해도 돼요/수영 금지예요.
suyeonghaedo dwaeyo/suyeong geumjiyeyo

Swimming is/is not supervised.
해수욕장에 관리인이 있어요/없어요.
haesuyokjange gwalliini isseoyo/eopseoyo

The water is warm/cold/freezing!
물이 따뜻해요/차가워요/얼음물이에요!
muri ttatteutaeyo/chagawoyo/eoreummurieyo

YOU SHOULD KNOW...

Public beaches are only monitored in summer. At the end of the summer, local authority lifeguards are no longer on duty and amenities are closed, although some surfers will still go to the beach.

VOCABULARY

seaside	"No swimming"	bathing zone
바닷가	"수영금지"	해수욕 가능 구역
badatga	suyeonggeumji	haesuyok ganeung guyeok

lifeguard
안전요원
anjeonyowon

surf zone
서핑전용해변
seopingjeonyonghaebyeon

to sunbathe
일광욕하다
ilgwangyokada

promenade
해안 산책로
haean sanchaengno

to surf
서핑하다
seopinghada

to swim
수영하다
suyeonghada

GENERAL

beach ball
비치 볼
bichi bol

bikini
비키니 수영복
bikini suyeongbok

bucket and spade
양동이와 삽
yangdongiwa sap

deckchair
갑판 의자
gappan uija

flip-flops
슬리퍼
seullipeo

flippers
오리발
oribal

hammock
해먹
haemeok

sandcastle
모래성
moraeseong

seashells
조개껍질
jogaekkeopjil

seaweed
해초
haecho

sunglasses
선글라스
seongeullaseu

sunhat
챙 넓은 모자
chaeng neolbeun moja

suntan lotion
태닝 로션
taening rosyeon

swimming trunks
남성용 수영복
namseongyong
suyeongbok

swimsuit
원피스 수영복
wonpiseu suyeongbok

THE SEASIDE

beach towel
해변용 수건
haebyeonyong
sugeon

sand
모래
morae

sea
바다
bada

waves
파도
pado

parasol
파라솔
parasol

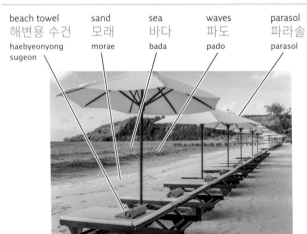

K-pop is the best-known genre of Korean music across the world, but it is not the only music the country has to offer. People also enjoy listening to various types of music such as hip hop, jazz, and classical music. Korean traditional music, known as 국악 (gugak), is also popular.

YOU MIGHT SAY...

I'm learning to play...
... 연주하는 걸 배우고
있어요.
... yeonjuhaneun geol baeugo isseoyo

What kind of music do you like?
어떤 음악을 좋아해요?
eotteon eumageul joahaeyo

YOU MIGHT HEAR...

I like/don't like...
... 좋아해요/안 좋아해요.
... joahaeyo/an joahaeyo

My favourite group is...
제가 가장 좋아하는 그룹은 ...
이에요/예요.
jega gajang joahaneun geurubeun ...
ieyo/yeyo

VOCABULARY

song
노래
norae

album
앨범
aelbeom

band
밴드
baendeu

singer-songwriter
가수겸 작곡가
gasugyeom jakgokga

live music
라이브 음악
raibeu eumak

gig
공연
gongyeon

CD
시디
sidi

DJ
디제이
dijei

vinyl record
레코드 음반
rekodeu eumban

turntable
턴테이블
teonteibeul

microphone
마이크
maikeu

K-pop
케이팝
keipap

pop
가요
gayo

rock
록
rok

rap
랩
raep

classical
클래식
keullaesik

to play an instrument
악기를 연주하다
akgireul yeonjuhada

to listen to music
음악을 듣다
eumageul deutda

folk
민요
minyo

to sing
노래하다
noraehada

to go to gigs
공연을 가다
gongyeoneul gada

EQUIPMENT

earphones
이어폰
ieopon

headphones
헤드폰
hedeupon

speakers
스피커
seupikeo

GENERAL MUSIC

choir
합창단
hapchangdan

conductor
지휘자
jihwija

musician
음악가
eumakga

orchestra
관현악단
gwanhyeonakdan

sheet music
악보
akbo

singer
가수
gasu

accordion
아코디언
akodieon

acoustic guitar
통기타
tonggita

bass drum
베이스 드럼
beiseu deureom

bass guitar
베이스 기타
beiseu gita

cello
첼로
chello

clarinet
클라리넷
keullarinet

cymbals
심벌즈
simbeoljeu

double bass
더블 베이스
deobeul beiseu

drum
드럼
deureom

electric guitar
전기 기타
jeongi gita

flute
플루트
peulluteu

harp
하프
hapeu

keyboard
키보드
kibodeu

mouth organ
하모니카
hamonika

piano
피아노
piano

saxophone
색소폰
saeksopon

trombone
트롬본
teurombon

trumpet
트럼펫
teureompet

tuba
튜바
tyuba

violin
바이올린
baiollin

xylophone
실로폰
sillopon

TRADITIONAL KOREAN INSTRUMENTS

double-headed drum
장구
janggu

Korean flute
단소
danso

Korean zither
가야금
gayageum

YOU MIGHT SAY...

Can I take photos here?
여기에서 사진 찍어도 돼요?
yeogieseo sajin jjigeodo dwaeyo

YOU MIGHT HEAR...

Say "kimchi"!
"김치" 하세요!
"gimchi" haseyo

VOCABULARY

photographer
사진사
sajinsa

photo
사진
sajin

selfie
셀카
selka

selfie stick
셀카봉
selkabong

to take a photo/selfie
사진을/셀카를 찍다
sajineul/selkareul jjikda

to zoom in
확대하다
hwakdaehada

camera lens
사진기 렌즈
sajingi renjeu

compact camera
컴팩트 카메라
keompaekteu kamera

drone
드론
deuron

DSLR camera
디에스엘아르
dieseuerareu

SD card
에스디 카드
eseudi kadeu

tripod
삼각대
samgakdae

Board games like "yunnori" and "go" are popular with the older generation, who like to go to community centres to meet up with friends and play together. Younger people tend to prefer computer and phone games.

YOU MIGHT SAY...

Shall we play a game?
우리 게임 할까요?
uri geim halkkayo

What would you like to play?
어떤 게임 하고 싶어요?
eotteon geim hago sipeoyo

How do you play?
어떻게 하는 거예요?
eotteoke haneun geoyeyo

YOU MIGHT HEAR...

It's your turn.
당신 차례예요.
dangsin charyeyeyo

Time's up!
시간 다 됐어요!
sigan da dwaesseoyo

Shall we play something else?
우리 다른 게임 할까요?
uri dareun geim halkkayo

VOCABULARY

player
참가자
chamgaja

poker
포커
pokeo

games console
게임기
geimgi

game controller
게임 조종기
geim jojonggi

video game
비디오 게임
bidio geim

virtual reality headset
가상 현실 헤드셋
gasang hyeonsil
hedeuset

draughts
체커
chekeo

hand (in cards)
수중의 패
sujungui pae

to play
게임하다
geimhada

to roll the dice
주사위를 던지다
jusawireul deonjida

to win
이기다
igida

to lose
지다
jida

board game
보드게임
bodeugeim

bowling
볼링
bolling

cards
카드
kadeu

chess
체스
cheseu

Chinese chess
장기
janggi

crossword
십자말풀이
sipjamalpuri

darts
다트
dateu

dice
주사위
jusawi

go
바둑
baduk

go-stop
고스톱
goseutop

jigsaw puzzle
퍼즐 맞추기
peojeul matchugi

yunnori
윷놀이
yunnori

Many Korean people enjoy different types of arts and crafts. While some enjoy Western arts and crafts, many traditional arts and crafts are still practised throughout the country.

VOCABULARY

handicrafts 수공예 sugongye	dressmaker 여성복 재봉사 yeoseongbok jaebongsa	to sew 바느질하다 baneujilhada
artist 예술가 yesulga	to paint 그림을 그리다 geurimeul geurida	to knit 뜨개질하다 tteugaejilhada
amateur 비전문가 bijeonmunga	to sketch 밑그림을 그리다 mitgeurimeul geurida	to be creative 창의적인 changuijeogin

GENERAL CRAFTS

calligraphy
서예
seoye

cross-stitch
십자수
sipjasu

embroidery
자수
jasu

jewellery-making
장신구 세공
jangsingu segong

model-making
프라모델 조립
peuramodel jorip

papercrafts
종이공예
jongigongye

pottery
도예
doye

traditional ink painting
수묵화
sumukwa

woodwork
목공예
mokgongye

ART MATERIALS

calligraphy brush
서예붓
seoyebut

canvas
캔버스
kaenbeoseu

easel
이젤
ijel

ink
잉크
ingkeu

oil paint
유화 물감
yuhwa mulgam

paintbrush
붓
but

palette
팔레트
palleteu

paper-cutting
종이 자르기
jongi jareugi

pastels
파스텔
paseutel

sketchpad
스케치북
seukechibuk

traditional black ink
먹물
meongmul

watercolours
수채화 물감
suchaehwa mulgam

SEWING ACCESSORIES

ball of wool
털실 뭉치
teolsil mungchi

button
단추
danchu

fabric
천
cheon

fabric scissors
재단 가위
jaedan gawi

knitting needles
뜨개바늘
tteugaebaneul

needle and thread
바늘과 실
baneulgwa sil

safety pin
옷핀
otpin

sewing machine
재봉틀
jaebongteul

tape measure
줄자
julja

172

SPORT | 운동

There are many opportunities to watch or take part in a range of sports in Korea. Baseball and football are popular in spring and summer, and the basketball and volleyball seasons are in autumn and winter. People gather in public spaces to watch international games together and enjoy supporting the national team.

football pitch
축구장
chukgujang

centre circle
센터 서클
senteo seokeul

penalty box
페널티 박스
peneolti bakseu

goal
골
gol

Where is...?
... 어디에 있어요?
... eodie isseoyo

Do you do any sports?
하는 운동이 있어요?
haneun undongi isseoyo

I play volleyball/football.
배구해요/축구해요.
baeguhaeyo/chukguhaeyo

Do you follow any sports?
챙겨보는 운동 경기가
있어요?
chaenggyeoboneun undong
gyeonggiga isseoyo

I'd like to book...
... 예약하고 싶어요.
... yeyakago sipeoyo

What's your favourite team?
어느 팀을 가장 좋아해요?
eoneu timeul gajang joahaeyo

VOCABULARY

tournament 토너먼트 toneomeonteu	sportsperson 운동선수 undongseonsu	to coach 지도하다 jidohada
competition 대회 daehoe	coach 코치 kochi	to compete 겨루다 gyeoruda
league 리그 rigeu	manager 감독 gamdok	to score 득점하다 deukjeomhada
champion 우승자 useungja	match 경기 gyeonggi	to win 이기다 igida
competitor 경쟁자 gyeongjaengja	points 점수 jeomsu	to lose 지다 jida
teammate 팀원 timwon	locker 사물함 samulham	to draw 비기다 bigida

changing room
탈의실
taruisil

leisure centre
공공 체육 시설
gonggong cheyuk siseol

medal
메달
medal

podium
시상대
sisangdae

referee
심판
simpan

scoreboard
득점 게시판
deukjeom gesipan

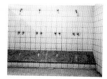

showers
샤워장
syawojang

spectators
관중
gwanjung

stadium
경기장
gyeonggijang

stands
관중석
gwanjungseok

team
팀
tim

trophy
우승컵
useungkeop

175

YOU MIGHT SAY...

I'd like to join the gym.
헬스장에 등록하고 싶어요.
helseujange deungnokago sipeoyo

I'd like to book a class.
수업을 예약하고 싶어요.
sueobeul yeyakago sipeoyo

What classes can you do here?
여기에서 어떤 수업을
해요?
yeogieseo eotteon sueobeul haeyo

YOU MIGHT HEAR...

Would you like to book an induction?
오리엔테이션을
예약하시겠어요?
orienteisyeoneul yeyakasigesseoyo

What time do you want to book for?
몇 시로 예약하시겠어요?
myeot siro yeyakasigesseoyo

We have 12 different classes.
12개의 다른 수업이 있어요.
yeoldugaeui dareun sueobi isseoyo

VOCABULARY

gym
헬스장
helseujang

gym instructor
헬스장 강사
helseujang gangsa

gym membership
헬스장 회원
helseujang hoewon

personal trainer
개인 트레이너
gaein teureineo

exercise class
운동 수업
undong sueop

to exercise
운동하다
undonghada

to keep fit
건강을 유지하다
geongangeul yujihada

to go for a run
조깅하다
joginghada

to go to the gym
헬스장에 가다
helseujange gada

THE GYM

cross trainer
크로스 트레이너
keuroseu teureineo

dumbbell
아령
aryeong

exercise bike
실내 자전거
sillae jajeongeo

gym ball
짐 볼
jim bol

kettlebell
케틀 벨
keteul bel

rowing machine
로잉 머신
roing meosin

skipping rope
줄넘기 줄
julleomgi jul

treadmill
러닝머신
reoningmeosin

weightlifting bench
웨이트 트레이닝 기구
weiteu teureining gigu

ACTIVITIES

Pilates
필라테스
pillateseu

press-ups
팔 굽혀 펴기
pal gupyeo pyeogi

running
달리기
dalligi

sit-ups
윗몸 일으키기
winmom ireukigi

weightlifting
웨이트 트레이닝
weiteu teureining

yoga
요가
yoga

Baseball is the most popular sport in Korea. The KBO league is the major baseball league and has a huge following. Baseball matches in Korea are family friendly and feature some entertaining chanting and singing.

VOCABULARY

baseball stadium 야구장 yagujang	home plate 홈 hom	mound 마운드 maundeu
batter 타자 taja	home run 홈런 homneon	pitcher 투수 tusu
catcher 포수 posu	inning 회 hoe	softball 소프트볼 sopeuteubol

baseball
야구공
yagugong

baseball bat
배트
baeteu

baseball cap
야구 모자
yagu moja

baseball game
야구 경기
yagu gyeonggi

baseball mitt
야구 글러브
yagu geulleobeu

baseball player
야구 선수
yagu seonsu

Basketball is a huge sport in Korea. People love watching NBA and KBL (the Korean equivalent). Korean people also love playing basketball, especially students; there are basketball courts in every school and university.

VOCABULARY

layup 레이업 슛 reieop syut	to play basketball 농구하다 nongguhada	to dribble 드리블하다 deuribeulhada
slam dunk 덩크 슛 deongkeu syut	to catch 잡다 japda	to block 막다 makda
free throw 자유투 jayutu	to throw 던지다 deonjida	to mark a player 선수를 전담 마크하다 seonsureul jeondam makeuhada

basket
바스켓
baseuket

basketball
농구공
nonggugong

basketball court
농구 코트
nonggu koteu

basketball game
농구 시합
nonggu sihap

basketball player
농구 선수
nonggu seonsu

basketball shoes
농구화
nongguhwa

FOOTBALL | 축구

Football is the second most popular sport in Korea, and there is a thriving domestic league, called the K-league. Many people enjoy watching the national team play, and Korean football fans also follow European league matches and the World Cup.

YOU MIGHT SAY...

Are you going to watch the match?
그 경기 볼 거예요?
geu gyeonggi bol geoyeyo

What's the score?
몇 대 몇이에요?
myeot dae myeochieyo

That was a foul!
반칙이었어요!
banchigieosseoyo

YOU MIGHT HEAR...

I'm watching the match.
그 경기 볼 거예요.
geu gyeonggi bol geoyeyo

The score is...
점수는 ... 대 ... 이에요/예요.
jeomsuneun ... dae ... ieyo/yeyo

Go on!
파이팅!
paiting

VOCABULARY

defender
수비수
subisu

striker
공격수
gonggyeoksu

substitute
교체 선수
gyoche seonsu

kick-off
경기 시작
gyeonggi sijak

half-time
중간 휴식 시간
junggan hyusik sigan

full-time
경기 종료
gyeonggi jongnyo

extra time
연장전
yeonjangjeon

injury time
추가 시간
chuga sigan

free kick
프리 킥
peuri kik

header
헤딩
heding

save
선방
seonbang

foul
반칙
banchik

offside	to play football	to tackle
오프사이드	축구하다	태클하다
opeusaideu	chukguhada	taekeulhada

penalty	to kick	to pass the ball
페널티	차다	공을 패스하다
peneolti	chada	gongeul paeseuhada

penalty box	to dribble	to score a goal
페널티 박스	드리블하다	골을 넣다
peneolti bakseu	deuribeulhada	goreul neota

football
축구공
chukgugong

football boots
축구화
chukguhwa

football match
축구 경기
chukgu gyeonggi

football pitch
축구 경기장
chukgu gyeonggijang

football player
축구 선수
chukgu seonsu

goal
골
gol

goalkeeper
골기퍼
golgipeo

whistle
호루라기
horuragi

yellow/red card
옐로/레드 카드
yello/redeu kadeu

RACKET SPORTS | 라켓 스포츠

Badminton is a popular sport in Korea. Tennis courts and table tennis tables can be found in some big city parks or leisure centres. It is often advisable to book them in advance.

VOCABULARY

ace
에이스
eiseu

rally
랠리
raelli

to play badminton
배드민턴을 치다
baedeuminteoneul chida

serve
서브
seobeu

singles
단식
dansik

to play squash
스쿼시를 치다
seukwosireul chida

backhand
백핸드
baekaendeu

doubles
복식
boksik

to hit
치다
chida

forehand
포핸드
pohaendeu

top seed
탑 시드 선수
tap sideu seonsu

to serve
서브하다
seobeuhada

fault
폴트
polteu

to play tennis
테니스를 치다
teniseureul chida

to break his/her serve
상대가 서브인
판에서 득점하다
sangdaega seobeuin
paneseo deukjeomhada

double fault
더블 폴트
deobeul polteu

BADMINTON

badminton
배드민턴
baedeuminteon

badminton racket
배드민턴 채
baedeuminteon chae

shuttlecock
셔틀콕
syeoteulkok

TENNIS

ball boy/girl
볼 보이/걸
bol boi/geol

line judge
선심판
seonsimpan

tennis
테니스
teniseu

tennis ball
테니스 공
teniseu gong

tennis court
테니스장
teniseujang

tennis player
테니스 선수
teniseu seonsu

tennis racket
테니스 채
teniseu chae

umpire
심판
simpan

umpire's chair
심판석
simpanseok

SQUASH

squash
스쿼시
seukwosi

squash ball
스쿼시 공
seukwosi gong

squash racket
스쿼시 채
seukwosi chae

183

WATER SPORTS | 수상 스포츠

There are a whole range of water sports you can try out whilst in Korea, on the coast as well as inland. In the summer months, many people enjoy rafting, waterskiing, and canoeing.

YOU MIGHT SAY...

Can I hire...?
... 빌릴 수 있어요?
... billil su isseoyo

I'm a keen swimmer.
저 수영 좋아해요.
jeo suyeong joahaeyo

YOU MIGHT HEAR...

You must wear a lifejacket.
구명조끼를 입으셔야 해요.
gumyeongjokkireul ibeusyeoya haeyo

You can hire...
... 빌릴 수 있어요.
... billil su isseoyo

VOCABULARY

breaststroke
평영
pyeongyeong

backstroke
배영
baeyeong

front crawl
자유형
jayuhyeong

butterfly
접영
jeobyeong

lane
레인
rein

length
세로 길이
sero giri

swimming lesson
수영 강습
suyeong gangseup

swimming
수영
suyeong

diving
다이빙
daibing

diver
다이빙 선수
daibing seonsu

angling
낚시
naksi

angler
낚시꾼
naksikkun

surfer
서핑하는 사람
seopinghaneun saram

to swim
수영하다
suyeonghada

to dive
다이빙하다
daibinghada

to surf
서핑하다
seopinghada

to paddle/row
노를 젓다
noreul jeotda

to fish
낚시하다
naksihada

armbands
팔 튜브
pal tyubeu

diving board
다이빙대
daibingdae

goggles
물안경
murangyeong

swimmer
수영 선수
suyeong seonsu

swimming cap
수영모
suyeongmo

swimming pool
수영장
suyeongjang

swimming trunks
남성용 수영복
namseongyong
suyeongbok

swimsuit
원피스 수영복
wonpiseu suyeongbok

water polo
수구
sugu

OPEN WATER

bodyboarding
보디보딩
bodiboding

canoeing
카누 타기
kanu tagi

jet ski®
제트 스키
jeteu seuki

kayaking
카약 타기
kayak tagi

lifejacket
구명조끼
gumyeongjokki

paddle
노
no

paddleboarding
패들보드 타기
paedeulbodeu tagi

rafting
래프팅
raepeuting

scuba diving
스쿠버 다이빙
seukubeo daibing

snorkelling
스노클링
seunokeulling

surfboard
서프보드
seopeubodeu

surfing
서핑
seoping

waterskiing
수상 스키 타기
susang seuki tagi

wetsuit
웨트슈트
weteusyuteu

windsurfing
윈드서핑
windeuseoping

Winter sports such as skiing or snowboarding are very popular in Korea. Half of the country is very mountainous and many of these mountains become ski resorts in winter.

YOU MIGHT SAY...

Can I hire some skis?
스키 빌릴 수 있어요?
seuki billil su isseoyo

I'd like a skiing lesson, please.
스키 강습을 듣고 싶어요.
seuki gangseubeul deutgo sipeoyo

I can't ski very well.
스키 잘 못 타요.
seuki jal mot tayo

What are the snow conditions like?
눈 상태가 어때요?
nun sangtaega eottaeyo

I've fallen.
넘어졌어요.
neomeojyeosseoyo

I've hurt myself.
다쳤어요.
dachyeosseoyo

YOU MIGHT HEAR...

You can hire skis here.
스키 빌릴 수 있어요.
seuki billil su isseoyo

You can book a skiing lesson here.
스키 강습 등록할 수 있어요.
seuki gangseup deungnokal su isseoyo

The piste is open/closed today.
활강코스 열었어요/닫았어요.
hwalgangkoseu yeoreosseoyo/dadasseoyo

The conditions are good/bad.
눈 상태 좋아요/나빠요.
nun sangtae joayo/nappayo

There's an avalanche risk.
눈사태 위험이 있어요.
nunsatae wiheomi isseoyo

Be careful.
조심하세요.
josimhaseyo

VOCABULARY

skiing
스키 타기
seuki tagi

snowboarding
스노보드 타기
seunobodeu tagi

skier
스키 타는 사람
seuki taneun saram

ski resort
스키장
seukijang

ski instructor
스키 강사
seuki gangsa

ski lift
리프트
ripeuteu

ice hockey
아이스 하키
aiseu haki

mountain rescue service
산악 구조대
sanak gujodae

first-aid kit
구급상자
gugeupsangja

snow
눈
nun

powder
가루눈
garunun

ice
얼음
eoreum

avalanche
눈사태
nunsatae

to ski (off-piste)
(활강코스 밖에서)
스키 타다
(hwalgangkoseu
bakkeseo) seuki tada

to snowboard
스노보드 타다
seunobodeu tada

to go mountain
climbing
등산 가다
deungsan gada

to go sledging
썰매 타러 가다
sseolmae tareo gada

GENERAL

crampons
아이젠
aijen

ice axe
얼음 도끼
eoreum dokki

ice skates
스케이트
seukeiteu

ice skating
스케이트 타기
seukeiteu tagi

rope
줄
jul

sledge
썰매
sseolmae

piste
활강코스
hwalgangkoseu

salopettes
스키바지
seukibaji

ski boots
스키화
seukihwa

ski gloves
스키 장갑
seuki janggap

ski goggles
스키 고글
seuki gogeul

ski helmet
스키 헬멧
seuki helmet

ski jacket
스키 재킷
seuki jaekit

ski poles
스키폴
seukipol

skis
스키
seuki

ski suit
원피스 스키복
wonpiseu seukibok

snowboard
스노보드
seunobodeu

snowboarding boots
스노보드 화
seunobodeu hwa

COMBAT SPORTS | 격투 스포츠

The best-known form of combat sport in Korea is taekwondo. Taekwondo focuses on agility and speed, with fast kicking techniques, and is one of the most popular martial arts in the world.

YOU MIGHT SAY...

I'd like to learn martial arts.
무술을 배우고 싶어요.
musureul baeugo sipeoyo

I'd like to learn some simple taekwondo moves.
간단한 태권도 기술을 배우고 싶어요.
gandanhan taekwondo gisureul baeugo sipeoyo

Where can I find a martial arts academy?
무술 도장이 어디에 있어요?
musul dojangi eodie isseoyo

YOU MIGHT HEAR...

There is a martial arts academy at...
무술 도장은 ... 에 있어요.
musul dojangeun ... e isseoyo

That teacher has been practising taekwondo for over 30 years.
선생님은 태권도를 30년 넘게 하셨어요.
seonsaengnimeun taekwondoreul samsipnyeon neomge hasyeosseoyo

Have you done taekwondo before?
태권도 해 본 적 있어요?
taegwondo hae bon jeok isseoyo

VOCABULARY

martial arts
무술
musul

martial arts academy
무술 도장
musul dojang

fight
대결
daegyeol

boxer
권투 선수
gwontu seonsu

fighter
격투 선수
gyeoktu seonsu

Korean wrestling
씨름
ssireum

opponent
상대 선수
sangdae seonsu

wrestling
레슬링
reseulling

fencing
펜싱
pensing

headguard
헤드기어
hedeugieo

mouthguard
마우스피스
mauseupiseu

to kick
차다
chada

190

to box
권투를 하다
gwontureul hada

to punch
치다
chida

to knock out
케이오 당하다
keio danghada

to wrestle
레슬링을 하다
reseullingeul hada

to spar
스파링하다
seuparinghada

BOXING

boxing gloves
권투 글러브
gwontu geulleobeu

boxing ring
권투 링
gwontu ring

punchbag
샌드백
saendeubaek

COMBAT SPORTS

aikido
합기도
hapgido

judo
유도
yudo

jujitsu
주짓수
jujitsu

kendo
검도
geomdo

kickboxing
킥복싱
kikboksing

taekwondo
태권도
taegwondo

More and more Korean people are starting to do athletics. Full or half marathon events are often held in big cities and there are usually a large number of participants.

VOCABULARY

runner
주자
juja

race
달리기 경주
dalligi gyeongju

marathon
마라톤
maraton

half marathon
하프마라톤
hapeumaraton

sprint
단거리 경주
dangeori gyeongju

relay
계주
gyeju

lane
레인
rein

start/finish line
출발선/결승선
chulbalseon/
gyeolseungseon

heat
예선
yeseon

final
결승전
gyeolseungjeon

triple jump
트리플 점프
teuripeul jeompeu

heptathlon
칠종 경기
chiljong gyeonggi

decathlon
십종 경기
sipjong gyeonggi

to do athletics
육상 스포츠를 하다
yuksang seupocheureul
hada

to run
달리다
dallida

to race
경주하다
gyeongjuhada

to jump
뛰어오르다
ttwieooreuda

to throw
던지다
deonjida

athlete
육상 선수
yuksang seonsu

discus
원반던지기
wonbandeonjigi

high jump
높이뛰기
nopittwigi

hurdles
장애물 달리기
jangaemul dalligi

javelin
투창
tuchang

long jump
멀리뛰기
meollittwigi

pole vault
장대높이뛰기
jangdaenopittwigi

running track
경주용 트랙
gyeongjuyong teuraek

shot put
투포환
tupohwan

spikes
스파이크 슈즈
seupaikeu syujeu

starting block
스타팅 블록
seutating beullok

stopwatch
스톱워치
seutobwochi

Cycling is becoming popular as a way of commuting and also as exercise. Central and local governments are encouraging the use of bicycles in order to reduce carbon emissions and to improve public health.

VOCABULARY

cycling jersey
자전거복
jajeongeobok

cycling shorts
자전거 반바지
jajeongeo banbaji

rider
자전거 타는 사람
jajeongeo taneun saram

road/track race
도로/트랙 종목
doro/teuraek jongmok

time trial
타임 트라이얼
taim teuraieol

stage
구간
gugan

to ride a bike
자전거를 타다
jajeongeoreul tada

to pedal
페달을 밟다
pedareul bapda

to crash
충돌하다
chungdolhada

BMX
비엠엑스
biemekseu

helmet
헬멧
helmet

mountain bike
산악 자전거
sanak jajeongeo

road bike
로드 바이크
rodeu baikeu

velodrome
경륜장
gyeongnyunjang

water bottle
물통
multong

VOCABULARY

minigolf
미니 골프
mini golpeu

green
그린
geurin

hole-in-one
홀인원
horinwon

golf course
골프장
golpeujang

bunker
벙커
beongkeo

over/under par
오버/언더 파
obeo/eondeo pa

clubhouse
클럽하우스
keulleopauseu

hole
홀
hol

to play golf
골프를 치다
golpeureul chida

caddie
캐디
kaedi

handicap
핸디캡
haendikaep

to tee off
티샷을 치다
tisyaseul chida

golf bag
골프 가방
golpeu gabang

golf ball
골프 공
golpeu gong

golf buggy
골프 카트
golpeu kateu

golf club
골프 채
golpeu chae

golfer
골프 선수
golpeu seonsu

tee
티
ti

archery
양궁
yanggung

climbing
암벽 등반
ambyeok deungban

equestrian
승마
seungma

fishing
낚시
naksi

gymnastics
체조
chejo

handball
핸드볼
haendeubol

hockey
하키
haki

shooting
사격
sagyeok

skateboarding
스케이트보드 타기
seukeiteubodeu tagi

snooker
스누커
seunukeo

table tennis
탁구
takgu

volleyball
배구
baegu

HEALTH | 건강

It's important to arrange appropriate cover for healthcare during your time in Korea. People staying in Korea for more than 6 months are automatically provided with national health insurance. If you are a short-term visitor, make sure that you have adequate health cover included in your travel insurance.

first-aid kit
구급 상자
gugeup sangja

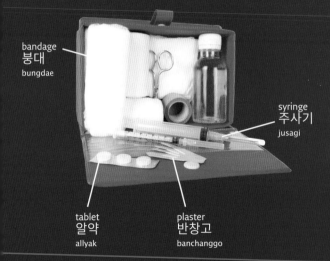

bandage
붕대
bungdae

syringe
주사기
jusagi

tablet
알약
allyak

plaster
반창고
banchanggo

The Korean health care system is different to the one in the UK. The pharmacy is usually the first port of call for most minor ailments. People who want to see a doctor go directly to a specialist in a private hospital.

YOU MIGHT SAY...

I don't feel well.
몸이 안 좋아요.
momi an joayo

I've hurt my...
... 을/를 다쳤어요.
... eul/reul dachyeosseoyo

I'm going to be sick.
속이 메스꺼워요.
sogi meseukkeowoyo

I need to see a doctor.
의사한테 가 봐야 해요.
uisahante ga bwaya haeyo

I need to go to hospital.
병원에 가야 해요.
byeongwone gaya haeyo

Call an ambulance.
구급차를 부르세요.
gugeupchareul bureuseyo

YOU MIGHT HEAR...

What's wrong?
왜 그래요?
wae geuraeyo

What are your symptoms?
증상이 어때요?
jeungsangi eottaeyo

Where does it hurt?
어디가 아파요?
eodiga apayo

How are you today?
오늘은 괜찮아요?
oneureun gwaenchanayo

How long have you been feeling like this?
언제부터 그랬어요?
eonjebuteo geuraesseoyo

VOCABULARY

nurse	specialist	paramedic
간호사	전문의	구급대원
ganhosa	jeonmunui	gugeupdaewon

pain
통증
tongjeung

symptom
증상
jeungsang

to be unwell
몸이 좋지 않다
momi jochi anta

illness
질병
jilbyeong

recovery
회복
hoebok

to recover
회복하다
hoebokada

mental health
정신 건강
jeongsin geongang

health insurance
의료 보험
uiryo boheom

to look after
보살피다
bosalpida

treatment
치료
chiryo

healthy
건강하다
geonganghada

to treat
치료하다
chiryohada

YOU SHOULD KNOW...

The national health insurance scheme covers 40-60% of any costs of private hospitals, with the remainder being paid by the individual.

doctor
의사
uisa

hospital
병원
byeongwon

medicine
약
yak

patient
환자
hwanja

pharmacist
약사
yaksa

pharmacy
약국
yakguk

VOCABULARY

throat 목구멍 mokgumeong	skin 피부 pibu	balance 균형 gyunhyeong
eyelash 속눈썹 songnunsseop	(body) hair 털 teol	to see 보다 boda
eyebrow 눈썹 nunsseop	height 키 ki	to smell 냄새 맡다 naemsae matda
eyelid 눈꺼풀 nunkkeopul	weight 체중 chejung	to hear 듣다 deutda
nostrils 콧구멍 kotgumeong	sense of hearing 청각 cheonggak	to touch 만지다 manjida
lips 입술 ipsul	sense of sight 시각 sigak	to taste 맛보다 matboda
tongue 혀 hyeo	sense of smell 후각 hugak	to stand 서다 seoda
breast 가슴 gaseum	sense of taste 미각 migak	to walk 걷다 geotda
genitals 생식기 saengsikgi	sense of touch 촉각 chokgak	to lose one's balance 균형을 잃다 gyunhyeongeul ilta

FACE

hair
머리카락
meorikarak

forehead
이마
ima

eye
눈
nun

ear
귀
gwi

cheek
볼
bol

nose
코
ko

mouth
입
ip

jaw
턱
teok

chin
턱끝
teokkkeut

HAND

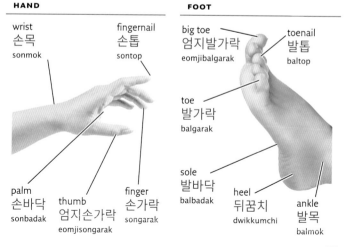

wrist
손목
sonmok

fingernail
손톱
sontop

palm
손바닥
sonbadak

thumb
엄지손가락
eomjisongarak

finger
손가락
songarak

FOOT

big toe
엄지발가락
eomjibalgarak

toenail
발톱
baltop

toe
발가락
balgarak

sole
발바닥
balbadak

heel
뒤꿈치
dwikkumchi

ankle
발목
balmok

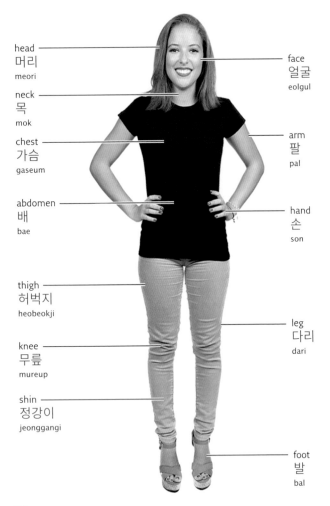

head
머리
meori

neck
목
mok

chest
가슴
gaseum

abdomen
배
bae

thigh
허벅지
heobeokji

knee
무릎
mureup

shin
정강이
jeonggangi

face
얼굴
eolgul

arm
팔
pal

hand
손
son

leg
다리
dari

foot
발
bal

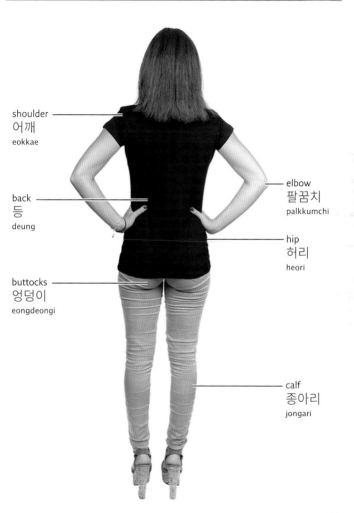

shoulder
어깨
eokkae

back
등
deung

buttocks
엉덩이
eongdeongi

elbow
팔꿈치
palkkumchi

hip
허리
heori

calf
종아리
jongari

VOCABULARY

skeleton
골격
golgyeok

kidney
신장
sinjang

bone
뼈
ppyeo

organ
장기
janggi

intestines
장
jang

muscle
근육
geunyuk

brain
뇌
noe

digestive system
소화 기관
sohwa gigwan

tendon
힘줄
himjul

heart
심장
simjang

respiratory system
호흡 기관
hoheup gigwan

tissue
조직
jojik

lung
폐
pye

bladder
방광
banggwang

cell
세포
sepo

liver
간
gan

blood
혈액
hyeoraek

artery
동맥
dongmaek

stomach
위
wi

joint
관절
gwanjeol

vein
정맥
jeongmaek

YOU SHOULD KNOW...

Parts of the body feature often in common Korean expressions, such as:

귀가 얇다 meaning "to be very gullible" (literally: to have thin ears)

발이 넓다 meaning "to be very sociable and have many acquaintances" (literally: to have wide feet)

혀는 칼보다 날카롭다 meaning "to say something that might cause someone harm" (literally: your tongue is sharper than a knife)

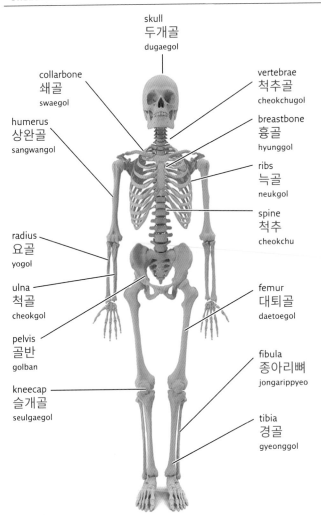

skull
두개골
dugaegol

collarbone
쇄골
swaegol

vertebrae
척추골
cheokchugol

humerus
상완골
sangwangol

breastbone
흉골
hyunggol

ribs
늑골
neukgol

spine
척추
cheokchu

radius
요골
yogol

ulna
척골
cheokgol

femur
대퇴골
daetoegol

pelvis
골반
golban

fibula
종아리뼈
jongarippyeo

kneecap
슬개골
seulgaegol

tibia
경골
gyeonggol

SEEING A DOCTOR | 병원 방문

If you need to see a doctor in Korea, you don't need to make an appointment in advance. You can either go to a hospital and ask to see a specialist, or go to a community health centre and ask to see a general doctor. However, you do have to pay a registration fee for this. Be aware that the "family doctor" concept doesn't exist in Korea. Doctors can, however, access a central database to see all prescriptions that have been issued to a patient.

YOU MIGHT SAY...

I'd like to see a doctor/specialist.
의사를/전문의를 보려고
하는데요.
uisareul/jeonmunuireul boryeogo
haneundeyo

I need to see a ... specialist.
... 전문의를 보려고
하는데요.
... jeonmunuireul boryeogo haneundeyo

I'm allergic to...
... 에 알레르기가 있어요.
... e allereugiga isseoyo

I take medication for...
... 약을 복용하고 있어요.
... yageul bogyonghago isseoyo

I've been feeling unwell.
몸이 계속 안 좋아요.
momi gyesok an joayo

YOU MIGHT HEAR...

May I examine you?
제가 진찰해도 될까요?
jega jinchalhaedo doelkkayo

Tell me if that hurts.
아프면 말씀하세요.
apeumyeon malsseumhaseyo

Do you have any allergies?
알레르기가 있어요?
allereugiga isseoyo

Do you take any medication?
복용 중인 약이 있어요?
bogyong jungin yagi isseoyo

You need to see a specialist.
전문의에게 가보셔야 해요.
jeonmunuiege gabosyeoya haeyo

VOCABULARY

clinic	examination	test
진료소	진찰	검사
jillyoso	jinchal	geomsa

prescription
처방
cheobang

antibiotics
항생제
hangsaengje

to examine
진찰하다
jinchalhada

vaccination
백신 접종
baeksin jeopjong

the pill
피임약
piimyak

to be on medication
약을 복용하다
yageul bogyonghada

medication
약물
yangmul

sleeping pill
수면제
sumyeonje

to be allergic to...
... 에 알레르기가
있다
... e allereugiga itda

blood pressure monitor
혈압계
hyeorapgye

examination room
진료실
jillyosil

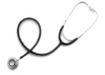

examination table
진찰대
jinchaldae

GP
일반의사
ilbanuisa

nurse
간호사
ganhosa

stethoscope
청진기
cheongjingi

syringe
주사기
jusagi

thermometer
체온계
cheongye

waiting room
대기실
daegisil

YOU MIGHT SAY...

Can I book an appointment?
예약을 할 수 있을까요?
yeyageul hal su isseulkkayo

I have toothache/an abscess.
치통이/염증이 있어요.
chitongi/yeomjeungi isseoyo

My filling has come out.
때운 게 떨어졌어요.
ttaeun ge tteoreojyeosseoyo

I've broken my tooth.
이가 부러졌어요.
iga bureojyeosseoyo

YOU MIGHT HEAR...

We don't have any appointments available.
예약이 다 찼어요.
yeyagi da chasseoyo

You need a new filling.
새로 때우셔야 해요.
saero ttaeusyeoya haeyo

Your tooth has to come out.
이를 뽑으셔야 해요.
ireul ppobeusyeoya haeyo

You need to have your teeth cleaned.
스케일링 하셔야 해요.
seukeilling hasyeoya haeyo

VOCABULARY

molar
어금니
eogeumni

incisor
앞니
amni

canine
송곳니
songgonni

wisdom teeth
사랑니
sarangni

filling
충전물
chungjeonmul

crown
크라운
keuraun

root canal treatment
신경치료
singyeongchiryo

toothache
치통
chitong

abscess
염증
yeomjeung

extraction
발치
balchi

to brush one's teeth
양치하다
yangchihada

to floss
치실질을 하다
chisiljireul hada

braces
치아 교정기
chia gyojeonggi

dental floss
치실
chisil

dental nurse
치과 간호사
chigwa ganhosa

dentist
치과 의사
chigwa uisa

dentist's chair
치과 의자
chigwa uija

dentist's drill
치과 천공기
chigwa cheongonggi

dentures
틀니
teulli

gums
잇몸
inmom

mouthwash
구강 세정제
gugang sejeongje

teeth
치아
chia

toothbrush
칫솔
chitsol

toothpaste
치약
chiyak

THE OPTICIAN'S | 안경점

Opticians are commercial businesses in Korea. If you want a pair of glasses, you go directly to the optician's. However, if you have a problem with your eyes, you need to go to the hospital and see an ophthalmologist.

YOU MIGHT SAY...

My eyes are dry/sore.
눈이 건조해요/아파요.
nuni geonjohaeyo/apayo

Do you repair glasses?
안경 수리 돼요?
angyeong suri dwaeyo

YOU MIGHT HEAR...

Look up/down/ahead.
위를/아래를/앞을 보세요.
wireul/araereul/apeul boseyo

You need reading glasses.
돋보기 안경을 쓰셔야 해요.
dotbogi angyeongeul sseusyeoya haeyo

VOCABULARY

ophthalmologist
안과 의사
angwa uisa

reading glasses
돋보기 안경
dotbogi angyeong

bifocals
이중 초점 안경
ijung chojeom angyeong

lens
렌즈
renjeu

conjunctivitis
결막염
gyeolmangnyeom

stye
다래끼
daraekki

blurred vision
시력 저하
siryeok jeoha

cataracts
백내장
baengnaejang

short-sighted
근시
geunsi

long-sighted
원시
wonsi

visually impaired
시각 장애
sigak jangae

blind
맹인
maengin

colour-blind
색맹
saengmaeng

to wear glasses
안경을 쓰다
angyeongeul sseuda

to use contacts
렌즈를 끼다
renjeureul kkida

contact lens case
콘택트 렌즈 보관 용기
kontaekteu renjeu bogwan yonggi

contact lenses
콘택트 렌즈
kontaekteu renjeu

eye chart
시력 검사표
siryeok geomsapyo

eye drops
점안액
jeomanaek

eye test
시력 검사
siryeok geomsa

frames
안경테
angyeongte

glasses
안경
angyeong

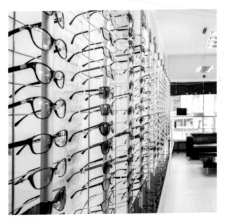

glasses case
안경집
angyeongjip

optician's
안경점
angyeongjeom

There are both public hospitals and private hospitals in Korea. The national insurance system covers both types. However, because it may still cost you if you have a serious illness, people tend to have additional private insurance to cover them for such situations.

YOU MIGHT SAY...

Which ward is ... in?
... 은/는 어느 병실에 있어요?
... eun/neun eoneu byeongsire isseoyo

What are the visiting hours?
병문안 시간이 어떻게 돼요?
byeongmunan sigani eotteoke dwaeyo

YOU MIGHT HEAR...

He/She is in ward...
... 병실에 계세요.
... byeongsire gyeseyo

Visiting hours are...
병문안 시간은 ... 예요.
byeongmunan siganeun ... yeyo

VOCABULARY

public hospital
공립 병원
gongnip byeongwon

private hospital
민간 병원
mingan byeongwon

A&E
응급실
eunggeupsil

ambulance
구급차
gugeupcha

physiotherapist
물리 치료사
mulli chiryosa

radiographer
방사선사
bangsaseonsa

surgeon
외과 의사
oegwa uisa

operation
수술
susul

scan
촬영
chwaryeong

intensive care
중환자실
junghwanjasil

diagnosis
진단
jindan

defibrillator
제세동기
jesedonggi

to take his/her pulse
맥박을 재다
maekbageul jaeda

to undergo surgery
수술을 받다
susureul batda

to be admitted/discharged
입원/퇴원하다
ibwon/toewonhada

crutches
목발
mokbal

drip
링거 주사
ringgeo jusa

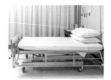

hospital bed
병원 침대
byeongwon chimdae

monitor
모니터
moniteo

neck brace
목 보호대
mok bohodae

operating theatre
수술실
susulsil

oxygen mask
산소 마스크
sanso maseukeu

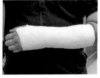

plaster cast
깁스
gipseu

ward
병실
byeongsil

wheelchair
휠체어
hwilcheeo

X-ray
엑스레이
ekseurei

Zimmer frame®
보행 보조기
bohaeng bojogi

YOU MIGHT SAY...

Can you help me?
저 좀 도와주실 수 있어요?
jeo jom dowajusil su isseoyo

Can you call an ambulance?
구급차 좀 불러 주시겠어요?
gugeupcha jom bulleo jusigesseoyo

I've had an accident.
사고를 당했어요.
sagoreul danghaesseoyo

I've hurt my...
... 을/를 다쳤어요.
... eul/reul dachyeosseoyo

I've broken my...
... 이/가 부러졌어요.
... i/ga bureojyeosseoyo

I've sprained my...
... 을/를 삐었어요.
... eul/reul ppieosseoyo

I've cut/burnt myself.
베었어요/데었어요.
beeosseoyo/deeosseoyo

I've hit my head.
머리를 부딪쳤어요.
meorireul buditchyeosseoyo

YOU MIGHT HEAR...

Do you feel faint?
어지러워요?
eojireowoyo

Do you feel sick?
토할 거 같아요?
tohal geo gatayo

I'm calling an ambulance.
구급차를 부를게요.
gugeupchareul bureulgeyo

Where does it hurt?
어디가 다쳤어요?
eodiga dachyeosseoyo

VOCABULARY

concussion 뇌진탕 noejintang	dislocation 탈골 talgol	scar 상처 sangcheo
accident 사고 sago	sprain 염좌 yeomjwa	whiplash 목뼈 부상 mokppyeo busang

swelling	stitches	to fall
부기	봉합	넘어지다
bugi	bonghap	neomeojida

recovery position	to injure oneself	to break one's arm
회복 자세	다치다	팔이 부러지다
hoebok jase	dachida	pari bureojida

CPR	to be unconscious	to twist one's ankle
심폐소생법	의식이 없다	발목을 삐다
simpyesosaengbeop	uisigi eopda	balmogeul ppida

YOU SHOULD KNOW...

The major phone numbers for emergency services in Korea are: 119 for
medical emergencies and the fire brigade; and 112 for the police.

INJURIES

blister
물집
muljip

bruise
타박상
tabaksang

burn
화상
hwasang

cut
절상
jeolsang

fracture
골절상
goljeolsang

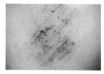

graze
찰과상
chalgwasang

splinter
가시 박힘
gasi bakim

sting
벌쏘임
beolssoim

sunburn
일광 화상
ilgwang hwasang

FIRST AID

adhesive tape
접착 테이프
jeopchak teipeu

bandage
붕대
bungdae

dressing
거즈
geojeu

first-aid kit
구급 상자
gugeup sangja

ice pack
얼음주머니
eoreumjumeoni

ointment
연고
yeongo

plaster
반창고
banchanggo

sling
팔걸이 붕대
palgeori bungdae

tweezers
핀셋
pinset

YOU MIGHT SAY...

I have a cold/the flu.
감기에/독감에 걸렸어요.
gamgie/dokgame geollyeosseoyo

I have a sore stomach/a rash/a fever.
복통이/발진이/열이 있어요.
boktongi/baljini/yeori isseoyo

I feel faint.
어지러워요.
eojireowoyo

I'm going to be sick.
토할 것 같아요.
tohal geot gatayo

I have asthma/diabetes.
천식이/당뇨가 있어요.
cheonsigi/dangnyoga isseoyo

YOU MIGHT HEAR...

You should go to the pharmacy/doctor.
약국에/병원에 가세요.
yakguge/byeongwone gaseyo

You need to rest.
쉬셔야 해요.
swisyeoya haeyo

Do you need anything?
필요한 거 있어요?
piryohan geo isseoyo

Take care of yourself.
몸 잘 챙겨요.
mom jal chaenggyeoyo

VOCABULARY

heart attack
심장마비
simjangmabi

virus
바이러스
baireoseu

stomach bug
장염
jangyeom

stroke
뇌졸중
noejoljung

cold
감기
gamgi

food poisoning
식중독
sikjungdok

infection
감염
gamnyeom

flu
독감
dokgam

vomiting
구토
guto

ear infection
중이염
jungiyeom

chicken pox
수두
sudu

diarrhoea
설사
seolsa

constipation
변비
byeonbi

diabetes
당뇨병
dangnyobyeong

epilepsy
간질
ganjil

asthma
천식
cheonsik

dizziness
현기증
hyeongijeung

inhaler
흡입기
heubipgi

period pain
생리통
saengnitong

to have high/low
blood pressure
고/저혈압
go/jeohyeorap

to cough
기침하다
gichimhada

to sneeze
재채기하다
jaechaegihada

to vomit
구토하다
gutohada

to faint
기절하다
gijeolhada

GENERAL

coughing
기침
gichim

fever
열
yeol

nausea
구역질
guyeokjil

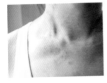

rash
발진
baljin

runny nose
콧물
konmul

sneezing
재채기
jaechaegi

PREGNANCY | 임신

If you are travelling to or in Korea while pregnant, make sure you have appropriate travel insurance in place.

YOU MIGHT SAY...

I'm (six months) pregnant.
임신 (6개월)이에요.
imsin (yukgaewol)ieyo

My partner/wife is pregnant.
배우자가/아내가 임신중이에요.
baeujaga/anaega imsinjungieyo

I'm/She's having contractions every ... minutes.
... 분마다 진통이 있어요.
... bunmada jintongi isseoyo

My/Her waters have broken.
양수가 터졌어요.
yangsuga teojyeosseoyo

I need pain relief.
무통 주사 놓아 주세요.
mutong jusa noa juseyo

YOU MIGHT HEAR...

How far along are you?
임신한 지 얼마나 되셨어요?
imsinhan ji eolmana doesyeosseoyo

How long is it between contractions?
진통이 몇 분 간격이에요?
jintongi myeot bun gangyeogieyo

Push!
힘 주세요!
him juseyo

Do you mind if I examine you?
제가 진찰해도 될까요?
jega jinchalhaedo doelkkayo

VOCABULARY

pregnant woman
임신부
imsinbu

foetus
태아
taea

uterus
자궁
jagung

cervix
자궁 경관
jagung gyeonggwan

labour
분만
bunman

epidural
경막외 주사
gyeongmagoe jusa

Caesarean section	stillborn	to be in labour
제왕 절개 수술	사산아	분만 중이다
jewang jeolgae susul	sasana	bunman jungida

delivery	due date	to give birth
출산	예정일	출산하다
chulsan	yejeongil	chulsanhada

newborn	morning sickness	to miscarry
신생아	입덧	유산하다
sinsaenga	ipdeot	yusanhada

miscarriage	to fall pregnant	to breast-feed
유산	임신하다	모유를 먹이다
yusan	imsinhada	moyureul meogida

GENERAL

incubator
인큐베이터
inkyubeiteo

labour suite
분만실
bunmansil

midwife
조산사
josansa

pregnancy test
임신 테스트
imsin teseuteu

sonographer
초음파 검사자
choeumpa geomsaja

ultrasound
초음파
choeumpa

ALTERNATIVE THERAPIES | 대체의학

Traditional Korean medicine has a long history, and many people find it effective
in treating chronic illnesses. To acquire a licence to practise Korean traditional
medicine, doctors must study for 6 years at university and then pass the
national exam. Only qualified doctors can open a clinic and offer treatments
such as acupuncture and herbal medicine.

VOCABULARY

therapist
치료사
chiryosa

reflexologist
반사 요법사
bansa yobeopsa

to relax
긴장을 풀다
ginjangeul pulda

masseur/masseuse
안마사
anmasa

Korean medicine
한의학
hanuihak

to massage
안마하다
anmahada

chiropractor
척추 지압사
cheokchu jiapsa

Korean medicine clinic
한의원
hanuiwon

to meditate
명상하다
myeongsanghada

acupuncturist
침술사
chimsulsa

doctor of Korean
medicine
한의사
hanuisa

acupuncture
침술
chimsul

chiropractic
척추 지압법
cheokchu jiapbeop

cupping therapy
부항 요법
buhang yobeop

essential oil
에센셜 오일
esensyeol oil

herbal medicine
한약
hanyak

hypnotherapy
최면 요법
choemyeon yobeop

massage
안마
anma

meditation
명상
myeongsang

moxibustion
뜸 요법
tteum yobeop

reflexology
반사 요법
bansa yobeop

osteopathy
정골 요법
jeonggol yobeop

thalassotherapy
해수 요법
haesu yobeop

If you intend to travel to Korea with your pet, your pet must be microchipped. It must also be over 3 months old and vaccinated against rabies at least 30 days prior to entering Korea. The UK is currently listed as a rabies-free country, but you should visit the relevant website for the latest updates.

YOU MIGHT SAY...

My dog has been hurt.
제 개가 다쳤어요.
je gaega dachyeosseoyo

My cat has been sick.
제 고양이가 아파요.
je goyangiga apayo

He/She keeps scratching.
얘가 계속 긁어요.
yaega gyesok geulgeoyo

My dog needs a tapeworm treatment.
제 개는 기생충 치료가 필요해요.
je gaeneun gisaengchung chiryoga piryohaeyo

YOU MIGHT HEAR...

Can you tell me what the problem is?
어떻게 오셨어요?
eotteoke osyeosseoyo

Has your dog been registered?
개가 등록되어 있어요?
gaega deungnokdoeeo isseoyo

Do you have a pet passport?
동물여권을 가지고 계세요?
dongmuryeogwoneul gajigo gyeseyo

Is he/she eating normally?
평소처럼 잘 먹나요?
pyeongsocheoreom jal meongnayo

YOU SHOULD KNOW...

Be aware that dogs are still not permitted in certain public areas, and even if they are, they should be kept on a lead at all times.

VOCABULARY

veterinary clinic
동물병원
dongmulbyeongwon

pet
애완동물
aewandongmul

flea
벼룩
byeoruk

tick
진드기
jindeugi

rabies vaccination
광견병 백신
gwanggyeonbyeong baeksin

pet passport
동물여권
dongmuryeogwon

quarantine
격리
gyeongni

to vaccinate
백신 접종을 하다
baeksin jeopjongeul hada

to spay/neuter
중성화하다
jungseonghwahada

microchip
마이크로칩
maikeurochip

to worm
기생충을 없애다
gisaengchungeul
eopsaeda

to put down
안락사하다
allaksahada

GENERAL

collar
애완동물 목걸이
aewandongmul mokgeori

E-collar
애완동물 넥카라
aewandongmul nekkara

lead
리드줄
rideujul

muzzle
입마개
immagae

pet carrier
이동장
idongjang

vet
수의사
suuisa

South Korea is mountainous, and offers dramatic and beautiful landscapes. The highland area, covering 14 mountain regions, is called Baekdudaegan, which means "big mountain ridge". It stretches from North Korea to the southern part of South Korea. The country is surrounded by three seas, boasts over 2,400 km of coastline, and has 3,000 islands. The biggest island, Jeju Island, is volcanic and is home to the tallest mountain in South Korea, Mt Hallasan (1,950 m).

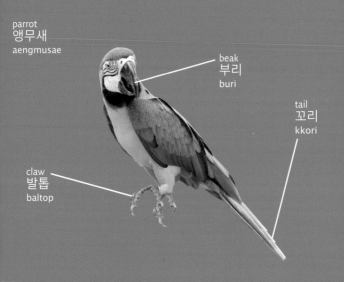

parrot
앵무새
aengmusae

beak
부리
buri

tail
꼬리
kkori

claw
발톱
baltop

YOU MIGHT SAY...

What is the scenery like?
경치가 어때요?
gyeongchiga eottaeyo

YOU MIGHT HEAR...

I'd recommend visiting...
... 에 가 보세요.
... e ga boseyo

VOCABULARY

nature reserve
자연 보호 구역
jayeon boho guyeok

hoof
발굽
balgup

wing
날개
nalgae

zoo
동물원
dongmurwon

snout
코
ko

beak
부리
buri

animal
동물
dongmul

mane
갈기
galgi

warm-blooded
온혈
onhyeol

species
종
jong

tail
꼬리
kkori

cold-blooded
냉혈
naenghyeol

fur
모피
mopi

claw
발톱
baltop

to bark
짖다
jitda

wool
양모
yangmo

horn
뿔
ppul

to purr
가르랑거리다
gareuranggeorida

paw
발
bal

feather
깃털
gitteol

to growl
으르렁거리다
eureureonggeorida

DOMESTIC ANIMALS AND BIRDS | 가축과 조류

Dogs, cats, and goldfish are the most popular pets in Korea. Cats and dogs must be microchipped and registered with the local council. Recently, the Korean term meaning "companion animal" has been encouraged instead of "pet".

YOU MIGHT SAY...

Do you have any pets?
키우는 동물이 있어요?
kiuneun dongmuri isseoyo

Is it OK to bring my pet?
제 애완동물을 데려와도
돼요?
je aewandongmureul deryeowado
dwaeyo

This is my guide dog/assistance dog.
얘는 제 안내견/
도우미견이에요.
yaeneun je annaegyeon/
doumigyeonieyo

What's the number for the vet?
동물병원 번호가 뭐예요?
dongmulbyeongwon beonhoga mwoyeyo

My pet is missing.
제 애완동물이 실종됐어요.
je aewandongmuri siljongdwaesseoyo

YOU MIGHT HEAR...

I have/don't have a pet.
애완동물이 있어요/없어요.
aewandongmuri isseoyo/eopseoyo

I'm allergic to pet hair.
동물 털에 알레르기가 있어요.
dongmul teore allereugiga isseoyo

Animals are/are not allowed.
동물 출입을 허가합니다/
금지합니다.
dongmul churibeul heogahamnida/
geumjihamnida

The phone number for the vet is...
동물병원 전화번호는 ...
이에요/예요.
dongmulbyeongwon
jeonhwabeonhoneun ... ieyo/yeyo

"Beware of the dog".
"개조심".
gaejosim

VOCABULARY

companion animal
반려동물
ballyeodongmul

companion dog
반려견
ballyeogyeon

companion cat
반려묘
ballyeomyo

pet
애완동물
aewandongmul

fish food
물고기 밥
mulgogi bap

cat litter
고양이 모래
goyangi morae

farmer
농부
nongbu

farm
농장
nongjang

farmland
농지
nongji

bull
수소
suso

rat
쥐
jwi

guide dog
안내견
annaegyeon

flock
떼
tte

herd
떼
tte

animal feed
사료
saryo

hay
건초
geoncho

straw
짚
jip

to have a pet
애완동물을 키우다
aewandongmuleul kiuda

to walk the dog
개를 산책시키다
gaereul sanchaeksikida

to go to the vet
수의사에게 가다
suuisaege gada

to farm
사육하다
sayukada

PETS

budgerigar
사랑앵무
sarangaengmu

canary
카나리아
kanaria

cat
고양이
goyangi

dog
개
gae

goldfish
금붕어
geumbungeo

guinea pig
기니피그
ginipigeu

hamster
햄스터
haemseuteo

parrot
앵무새
aengmusae

rabbit
토끼
tokki

FARM ANIMALS

chicken
닭
dak

cow
암소
amso

donkey
당나귀
dangnagwi

duck
오리
ori

goat
염소
yeomso

goose
거위
geowi

horse
말
mal

pig
돼지
dwaeji

sheep
양
yang

calf
송아지
songaji

cub
육식 동물 새끼
yuksik dongmul saekki

fawn
새끼 사슴
saekki saseum

foal
망아지
mangaji

kid
새끼 염소
saekki yeomso

kitten
새끼 고양이
saekki goyangi

lamb
새끼 양
saekki yang

piglet
새끼 돼지
saekki dwaeji

puppy
강아지
gangaji

aquarium
수족관
sujokgwan

barn
헛간
heotgan

birdcage
새장
saejang

cage
우리
uri

dog basket
반려견 방석
ballyeogyeon bangseok

hutch
사육장
sayukjang

kennel
개집
gaejip

litter tray
고양이 배변판
goyangi baebyeonpan

pet bowl
애완동물 식기
aewandongmul sikgi

pet food
애완동물 사료
aewandongmul saryo

stable
외양간
oeyanggan

trough
여물통
yeomultong

badger
오소리
osori

bat
박쥐
bagjwi

boar
멧돼지
metdwaeji

deer
사슴
saseum

fox
여우
yeou

hare
산토끼
santokki

hedgehog
고슴도치
goseumdochi

mole
두더지
dudeoji

mouse
생쥐
saengjwi

otter
수달
sudal

squirrel
다람쥐
daramjwi

wolf
늑대
neukdae

OTHER COMMON MAMMALS

bear
곰
gom

camel
낙타
nakta

chimpanzee
침팬지
chimpaenji

elephant
코끼리
kokkiri

giant panda
대왕판다
daewangpanda

giraffe
기린
girin

hippopotamus
하마
hama

kangaroo
캥거루
kaenggeoru

lion
사자
saja

monkey
원숭이
wonsungi

rhinoceros
코뿔소
koppulso

tiger
호랑이
horangi

blackbird
찌르레기
jjireuregi

buzzard
말똥가리
malttonggari

crane
두루미
durumi

crow
까마귀
kkamagwi

dove
흰 비둘기
huin bidulgi

eagle
수리
suri

finch
콩새
kongsae

flamingo
홍학
honghak

gull
갈매기
galmaegi

heron
왜가리
waegari

kingfisher
물총새
mulchongsae

lark
종달새
jongdalsae

magpie
까치
kkachi

ostrich
타조
tajo

owl
부엉이
bueongi

peacock
공작새
gongjaksae

pelican
사다새
sadasae

penguin
펭귄
penggwin

pigeon
비둘기
bidulgi

sparrow
참새
chamsae

stork
황새
hwangsae

swan
백조
baekjo

thrush
지빠귀
jippagwi

vulture
독수리
doksuri

VOCABULARY

tadpole
올챙이
olchaengi

scales
비늘
bineul

to hiss
쉬익하는 소리를
내다
swiikaneun sorireul naeda

frogspawn
개구리알
gaegurial

shell
껍질
kkeopjil

to croak
개골개골 울다
gaegolgaegol ulda

alligator
악어
ageo

frog
개구리
gaeguri

gecko
도마뱀붙이
domabaembuchi

lizard
도마뱀
domabaem

newt
도롱뇽
dorongnyong

snake
뱀
baem

toad
두꺼비
dukkeobi

tortoise
거북
geobuk

turtle
바다거북
badageobuk

coral
산호
sanho

crab
게
ge

dolphin
돌고래
dolgorae

eel
장어
jangeo

jellyfish
해파리
haepari

killer whale
범고래
beomgorae

lobster
바닷가재
badatgajae

seal
바다표범
badapyobeom

sea urchin
성게
seongge

shark
상어
sangeo

starfish
불가사리
bulgasari

whale
고래
gorae

VOCABULARY

swarm
떼
tte

cobweb
거미집
geomijip

to buzz
윙윙 거리다
wingwing georida

colony
군집
gunjip

insect bite
곤충 교상
gonchung gyosang

to sting
쏘다
ssoda

ant
개미
gaemi

bee
벌
beol

beetle
딱정벌레
ttakjeongbeolle

butterfly
나비
nabi

caterpillar
애벌레
aebeolle

centipede
지네
jine

cockroach
바퀴벌레
bakwibeolle

cricket
귀뚜라미
gwitturami

dragonfly
잠자리
jamjari

earthworm
지렁이
jireongi

fly
파리
pari

grasshopper
메뚜기
mettugi

ladybird
무당벌레
mudangbeolle

mayfly
하루살이
harusari

mosquito
모기
mogi

moth
나방
nabang

slug
민달팽이
mindalpaengi

snail
달팽이
dalpaengi

spider
거미
geomi

wasp
말벌
malbeol

woodlouse
쥐며느리
jwimyeoneuri

VOCABULARY

stalk 줄기 julgi	pollen 꽃가루 kkotgaru	grass 잔디 jandi
leaf 잎 ip	bud 싹 ssak	seed 씨 ssi
petal 꽃잎 kkonnip	wildflower 들꽃 deulkkot	bulb 구근 gugeun

YOU SHOULD KNOW...

Some flowers have cultural connotations in Korea – the carnation symbolizes gratitude and admiration, and people buy them for their parents on Parents' Day and for teachers on Teacher's Day. White chrysanthemums are usually used as cemetery flowers.

calla lily
칼라
kalla

carnation
카네이션
kaneisyeon

chrysanthemum
국화
gukwa

daffodil
수선화
suseonhwa

daisy
데이지
deiji

dandelion
민들레
mindeulle

gypsophila
안개꽃
angaekkot

iris
아이리스
airiseu

jasmine
재스민
jaeseumin

lily
백합
baekap

lily-of-the-valley
은방울꽃
eunbangulkkot

orchid
난초
nancho

peony
작약
jagyak

poppy
양귀비
yanggwibi

rose
장미
jangmi

rose of sharon
무궁화
mugunghwa

sunflower
해바라기
haebaragi

tulip
튤립
tyullip

VOCABULARY

tree
나무
namu

orchard
과수원
gwasuwon

branch
가지
gaji

plant
화초
hwacho

vineyard
포도원
podowon

berry
베리
beri

bamboo
대나무
daenamu

camphor tree
녹나무
nongnamu

cherry tree
벚꽃나무
beotkkonnamu

chestnut
밤나무
bamnamu

cypress
편백나무
pyeonbaengnamu

fir
전나무
jeonnamu

fungus
균류
gyullyu

grapevine
포도 덩굴
podo deonggul

honeysuckle
인동
indong

ivy
담쟁이덩굴
damjaengideonggul

lavender
라벤더
rabendeo

lichen
지의류
jiuiryu

lilac
라일락
raillak

maidenhair tree
은행나무
eunhaengnamu

maple
단풍나무
danpungnamu

moss
이끼
ikki

oak
참나무
chamnamu

pine
소나무
sonamu

plane
버즘나무
beojeumnamu

poplar
미루나무
mirunamu

willow
버드나무
beodeunamu

243

VOCABULARY

landscape 지형 jihyeong	estuary 어귀 eogwi	rural 전원 jeonwon
soil 땅 ttang	air 공기 gonggi	urban 도시 dosi
mud 진흙 jinheuk	atmosphere 대기 daegi	polar 극지방 geukjibang
water 물 mul	comet 혜성 hyeseong	tropical 열대지방 yeoldaejibang

LAND

cave
동굴
donggul

desert
사막
samak

farmland
농지
nongji

forest
산림
sallim

glacier
빙하
bingha

grassland
초원
chowon

hill
언덕
eondeok

lake
호수
hosu

marsh
습지
seupji

mountain
산
san

pond
연못
yeonmot

river
강
gang

rocks
바위
bawi

scrub
관목 덤불
gwanmok deombul

stream
개울
gaeul

valley
골짜기
goljjagi

volcano
화산
hwasan

waterfall
폭포
pokpo

SEA

cliff
절벽
jeolbyeok

coast
해안
haean

coral reef
산호초
sanhocho

island
섬
seom

peninsula
반도
bando

rock pool
조수 웅덩이
josu ungdeongi

SKY

aurora
오로라
orora

moon
달
dal

rainbow
무지개
mujigae

stars
별
byeol

sun
해
hae

sunset
일몰
ilmol

CELEBRATIONS AND FESTIVALS | 명절과 축제

Everyone loves having a reason to get together and celebrate. In Korea, this usually means great food and the company of close family and friends. Some Western holidays like Christmas and Halloween are celebrated more and more in Korea, although they don't bear quite the same cultural and religious significance as they do in the West. There is also a wealth of Korean customs and traditions associated with the various holidays and festivals throughout the year.

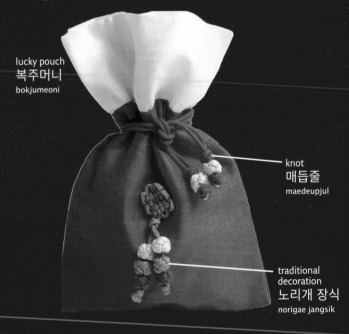

lucky pouch
복주머니
bokjumeoni

knot
매듭줄
maedeupjul

traditional
decoration
노리개 장식
norigae jangsik

In Korea, annual birthday parties are normally for children, while adults usually only celebrate the "big" ones like 60, 70, and so on.

YOU MIGHT SAY/HEAR...

Congratulations!
축하해요!
chukahaeyo

Happy anniversary!
기념일 축하해요!
ginyeomil chukahaeyo

Well done!
잘했어요!
jalhaesseoyo

Best wishes.
행운을 기원합니다.
haenguneul giwonhamnida

Cheers!
건배!
geonbae

Thank you.
감사합니다.
gamsahamnida

Happy birthday!
생일 축하해요!
saengnil chukahaeyo

You're very kind.
참 친절하시네요.
cham chinjeolhasineyo

VOCABULARY

celebration
축하
chuka

wedding anniversary
결혼 기념일
gyeolhon ginyeomil

special occasion
특별한 행사
teukbyeolhan haengsa

birthday
생일
saengnil

public holiday
공휴일
gonghyuil

good news
좋은 소식
joeun sosik

anniversary
기념일
ginyeomil

religious festival
종교 축제
jonggyo chukje

bad news
나쁜 소식
nappeun sosik

to celebrate	to throw a party	to toast
축하하다	파티를 열다	건배하다
chukahada	patireul yeolda	geonbaehada

YOU SHOULD KNOW...

A Korean child's first birthday is very important and features an interesting fortune-telling ritual known as 돌잡이 (doljabi). This involves placing different items in front of the child for them to grab. Whichever one the child decides to go for bears symbolic meaning as to what kind of career they are going to embrace in the future.

FIRST BIRTHDAY

bouquet
꽃다발
kkotdabal

box of chocolates
초콜릿 박스
chokollit bakseu

cake
케이크
keikeu

decorations
장식품
jangsikpum

fireworks
불꽃놀이
bulkkonnori

fizzy drink
탄산음료
tansaneumnyo

greetings card
인사 카드
insa kadeu

gift
선물
seonmul

party
파티
pati

LIFE EVENTS | 인생에서 겪는 큰 일

It is customary to give money rather than gifts on both happy and sad occasions. Celebration money is called 축의금 (chuguigeum), and condolence money is known as 조의금 (jouigeum) – both are presented in a white envelope.

VOCABULARY

birth
출생
chulsaeng

graduation
졸업
joreop

divorce
이혼
ihon

100-day celebration
백일잔치
baegiljanchi

finding a job
구직
gujik

having a child
아이를 갖는 것
aireul ganneun geot

first day of school
등교 첫 날
deunggyo cheot nal

engagement
약혼
yakon

retirement
은퇴
euntoe

passing your driving test
운전면허 시험 통과
unjeonmyeonheo siheom tonggwa

marriage
결혼
gyeolhon

funeral
장례
jangnye

YOU SHOULD KNOW...

A Korean baby's 100-day celebration is very important since it marks the first time that the baby is introduced to the world. The celebration used to involve a banquet and a huge party with family and friends. Nowadays, people often prefer having a small party with only immediate family attending.

In Korea, there are 14 annual public holidays, each of which involves large-scale celebrations. There are also seasonal and local festivals, such as the Cherry Blossom Festival, that attract thousands of people. Dano 단오 (dano) is not a public holiday in Korea, but is traditionally celebrated; the Gangneung Danoje Festival - designated by UNESCO as an Intangible Cultural Heritage of Humanity - is an example of this.

YOU MIGHT SAY/HEAR...

How many days' holiday do we get?
우리 며칠 쉬어요?
uri myeochil swieoyo

Is it a holiday today?
오늘 휴일이에요?
oneul hyuirieyo

What are you celebrating today?
오늘 무슨 특별한 날이에요?
oneul museun teukbyeolhan narieyo

I wish you...
... 를 바라요.
reul barayo

Merry Christmas!
성탄절 잘 보내세요!
seongtanjeol jal bonaeseyo

Happy New Year!
새해 복 많이 받으세요!
saehae bok mani badeuseyo

Happy holidays!
휴일 잘 보내세요!
hyuil jal bonaeseyo

And to you, too!
당신도요!
dangsindoyo

What are your plans for the holiday?
휴일에 뭐 할 거예요?
hyuire mwo hal geoyeyo

VOCABULARY

Parents' Day
어버이날
eobeoinal

National Day
국경일
gukgyeongil

May Day
근로자의 날
geullojaui nal

Father Christmas/
Santa Claus
산타클로스
santakeulloseu

Christmas Day
성탄절
seongtanjeol

Christmas Eve
성탄절 전야
seongtanjeol jeonya

New Year's Day	Halloween	Valentine's Day
신정	핼러윈	밸런타인데이
sinjeong	haelleowin	baelleontaindei

YOU SHOULD KNOW...

On national holidays and anniversaries in Korea, people hang the Korean flag outside their houses. This is done to commemorate particular days, for example: March First Independence Movement (3.1 절 sam.iljeol); Constitution Day (제헌절 jeheonjeol); National Liberation Day (광복절 gwangbokjeol); National Foundation Day (개천절 gaecheonjeol); and Hangul Proclamation Day (한글날 hangeullal).

OTHER FESTIVALS

Buddha's Birthday
석가 탄신일
seokga tansinil

Cherry Blossom Festival
벚꽃 축제
beotkkot chukje

Children's Day
어린이날
eorininal

Christmas
성탄절
seongtanjeol

Danoje Festival
단오제
danoje

First Full Moon Day
정월 대보름
jeongwol daeboreum

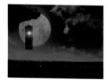

Harvest Festival
추석
chuseok

Lantern Festival
유등 축제
yudeung chukje

Lunar New Year
설날
seollal

National Liberation Day
광복절
gwangbokjeol

New Year's Eve
제야
jeya

Ramadan
라마단
ramadana

Most traditional Korean holidays are associated with particular dishes. These include: rice cake soup for Lunar New Year; five-grain rice and nuts and flavoured glutinous rice for First Full Moon Day, usually served with seasoned vegetables; and rice cakes with sweet fillings for Harvest Festival.

ancestral rites food
차례 음식
charye eumsik

five-grain rice and nuts
오곡밥과 견과류
ogokbapgwa gyeongwaryu

flavoured glutinous rice
약식
yaksik

rice cake soup
떡국
tteokguk

rice cake with sweet filling
송편
songpyeon

seasoned vegetables
나물
namul

YOU SHOULD KNOW...

Some festival foods have a special meaning. For example, eating rice cake soup on Lunar New Year means that you wish for your family to have long and healthy lives; and cracking nuts on First Full Moon Day symbolizes your wishes for a peaceful year ahead.

KOREAN FESTIVAL CUSTOMS | 명절 풍속

Lunar New Year and Harvest Festival are the most important celebrations of the year for Koreans, and many people return to their hometown to spend time with family. Ancestors are honoured through ancestral rites, with freshly harvested rice and vegetables prepared for the table, and gifts are exchanged.

YOU MIGHT SAY/HEAR...

Best wishes for Harvest Festival.
즐거운 한가위 되세요.
jeulgeoun hangawi doeseyo

Are you going home for Harvest Festival this year?
이번 추석에 고향에 내려가요?
ibeon chuseoge gohyange naeryeogayo

ancestral grave visit
성묘
seongmyo

ancestral rites
차례
charye

Full Moon viewing
달맞이
dalmaji

holiday migration
명절 대이동
myeongjeol daeidong

Korean traditional clothing
한복
hanbok

New Year's bow
세배
sebae

YOU SHOULD KNOW...

The New Year's bow, 세배 (sebae), is a traditional ritual carried out at Lunar New Year. People typically wear traditional Korean dress, 한복 (hanbok), and wish their elders a happy new year by performing a traditional bow. In return, elders usually give children and young people money and a word of wisdom.

abalone 91
abdomen 202
ABOUT YOU 9
accessories 107
accordion 165
acoustic guitar 165
acupuncture 221
adhesive tape 216
aerial 54
aeroplane 44
aikido 191
airbag 32
air bed 159
airport 44
AIR TRAVEL 42
alarm clock 65
alligator 236
ALTERNATIVE
    THERAPIES 221
aluminium foil 59
AMPHIBIANS AND
    REPTILES 236
ancestral grave visit
    256
ancestral rites 256
ancestral rites food
    255
anchor 47
anchovy 90
ankle 201
ant 238
antifreeze 32
antiperspirant 100
antique shop 115
antiseptic cream 98
apple 84
apricot 84
aquarium 231
archery 196
arm 202
armbands 185
art gallery 151
ARTS AND CRAFTS
    170
asparagus 86
athlete 192
ATHLETICS 192
ATM 142
AT THE SHOPS 73
aubergine 86
aurora 246
baby bath 103
baby food 102
BABY GOODS 102

Babygro® 102
baby's bottle 102
baby shoes 102
baby sling 103
back 203
bacon 93
badger 232
badminton 182
badminton racket
    182
baggage reclaim 44
baguette 95
BAKERY AND
    PATISSERIE 94
BALCONY 69
balcony 49
ball boy 183
ballet 153
ball girl 183
ball of wool 172
bamboo 242
bamboo shoots 86
banana 73, 84
bandage 98, 197, 216
BANK 141
banknotes 76, 142
bar 127, 153
barbecued pork belly
    122
barber's 115
barn 231
BASEBALL 178
baseball 178
baseball bat 178
baseball cap 111, 178
baseball game 178
baseball mitt 178
baseball player 178
BASICS 8, 20, 50, 74,
    118, 148, 174, 198,
    226, 248
basket 73, 78, 179
BASKETBALL 179
basketball 179
basketball court 179
basketball game 179
basketball player 179
basketball shoes 179
bass drum 165
bass guitar 165
bat 232
bath 68
BATHROOM 67
BEACH 160

beach ball 161
beach towel 162
beak 225
bear 233
beauty salon 115
BEAUTY SHOP 100
bed 66
bedding 65
BEDROOM 65
bedside lamp 66
bedside table 66
bee 238
beefburger 93
beer 80
beer mug 127
beetle 238
bell 37
belt 111
bib 102
BICYCLE 36
big toe 201
bike lock 37
bikini 109, 161
bill 127
bin bag 71, 76
birdcage 70, 231
BIRDS 234
biscuits 78
black 7
blackbird 234
black pudding 130
blade 19
blister 215
block of flats 49
blood pressure
    monitor 207
blouse 109
blue 7
blueberry 84
blusher 101
BMX 194
boar 232
board game 169
boarding card 44
BODY 200
bodyboarding 185
boiler 53
bonnet 26
book 104
bookcase 57
bookshop 115
boot 26
boots 35
bouquet 250

bow 48
bowling 169
box 144
boxing gloves 191
boxing ring 191
box of chocolates
    250
bracelet 111
braces 209
braised beef ribs 122
braised chicken 122
braised pork 122
brake 37
bread 73
bread rolls 95
BREAKFAST 119
breastbone 205
bridge 28
broccoli 86
bruise 215
brush 71
bubble wrap 144
bucket 71
bucket and spade
    161
Buddha's Birthday
    253
budgerigar 228
bumper 26
bungalow 51
buoy 47
bureau de change
    142
burger 130
burn 215
BUS 33
bus 34
busking 153
BUTCHER'S 92
butter 96
butterfly 238
buttocks 203
buttons 172
buzzard 234
cabbage 86
cabin 25
cabinet 68
cable 132
café 145
cage 231
cake 250
calf 203, 230
calla lily 240
calligraphy 170

calligraphy brush 171
camel 233
camera 151
camera lens 167
camphor tree 242
CAMPING 158
camping stove 159
campus 137
canal boat 48
canary 228
canoeing 185
cantaloupe 84
canteen 137
canvas 171
capsule 98
CAR 22
caravan 159
card reader 76
cards 169
carnation 240
carp 90
car park 28
carriage 40
carrot 86
car showroom 115
CAR TROUBLE 30
car wash 28
casino 154
casserole dish 60
cat 228
caterpillar 238
cauliflower 87
cave 244
ceiling fan 53
CELEBRATIONS AND
    FESTIVALS 247
celery 87
cello 165
centipede 238
centre circle 173
cereal 119
chain 37
chair 127
changing bag 102
changing room 175
charger 132
check-in desk 45
cheek 201
cherry 84
Cherry Blossom
    Festival 253
cherry tree 242
chess 169
chest 202

chestnut 242
chest of drawers 66
chicken 229
Children's Day 253
chilli 87
chimney 54
chimpanzee 233
chin 201
Chinese cabbage 87
Chinese chess 169
chiropractic 221
chocolate 80
chocolate spread 119
choir 164
chopping board 60
chopsticks 64, 128
Christmas 254
chrysanthemum 240
church 145
cigarette 104
cinema 154, 154
city map 151
clam 91
clarinet 165
classroom 135
claw 225
cliff 246
climbing 196
clingfilm 59
cloth 71
clothes horse 71
clothes pegs 71
CLOTHING AND
   FOOTWEAR 108
coach 34
coast 246
coat 109
coat hanger 65
cockpit 19, 45
cockroach 238
cod 90
coffee 119
coffee with milk 117,
   119
coins 76
colander 60
cold noodles 122
collar 224
collarbone 205
colouring pencils 135
comb 101
COMBAT SPORTS 190
comic book 104
COMMUNICATION AND
   IT 131
compact camera 167
computer 132
concert 154
conditioner 100
condom 99

conductor 164
confectionery 104
conference centre
   145
contact lens case 211
contact lenses 211
convenience store
   115
cooker hood 60
cooking 149
cool box 159
coral 237
coral reef 246
corridor 157
cosmetics 107
cot 103
cotton bud 103
cotton wool 103
couchette 40
coughing 218
cough mixture 99
courgette 87
courthouse 145
court shoes 112
courtyard house 51
cow 229
crab 91, 237
crampons 188
crane 234
crash helmet 35
crate 82
cream 96
credit card 76, 142
cricket 238
crisps 80
croissant 95
crossbar 37
cross-stitch 170
crosstalk 154
cross trainer 176
crossword 169
crow 234
crutches 213
cub 230
cucumber 87
cup 117
cupboard 62
cup noodle 130
cupping therapy 221
curtains 57, 66
cushion 58
customer 82
cut 215
CYCLING 194
cymbals 165
cypress 242
daffodil 240
daisy 240
dandelion 240
Danish pastry 95

Danoje Festival 254
darts 169
dashboard 24
DAYS, MONTHS, AND
   SEASONS 16
DAY-TO-DAY 117
debit card 76, 142
deck 48
deckchair 161
decking 54
decorations 250
deer 232
dental floss 209
dental nurse 209
dentist 209
dentist's chair 209
dentist's drill 209
DENTIST'S SURGERY
   208
dentures 209
DEPARTMENT STORE
   106
department store 115
departure board 40
desert 244
desk 139
detached house 51
dice 169
DINING ROOM 63
discus 192
display cabinet 57
diving board 185
DIY 149
doctor 199
dog 228
dog basket 231
dolphin 237
DOMESTIC ANIMALS
   AND BIRDS 227
donkey 229
"do not disturb" sign
   157
door 26
doorbell 56
door handle 56
doormat 56
double bass 165
double-headed drum
   166
double room 157
doughnut 95
dove 234
dragonfly 238
draining board 62
drainpipe 54
drawer 62
dressing 216
dressing gown 110
dressing table 65
dried persimmon 124

drill 113
drip 213
driveway 54
DRIVING 27
drone 167
drops 99
drum 165
dry cleaner's 145
DSLR camera 167
duck 229
dumbbell 176
dumplings 122
dungarees 110
dustpan 72
duty-free shop 45
duvet 66

eagle 234
ear 201
earphones 164
earrings 112
earthworm 239
easel 171
EATING OUT 125
éclair 95
E-collar 224
EDUCATION 134
eel 90, 237
egg 96
elbow 203
electrical retailer 115
electric guitar 165
electric rice cooker
   60
elephant 233
embroidery 170
ENTRANCE 55
envelope 104, 144
equestrian 196
eraser 135
essential oil 222
ESSENTIALS 7
estate agency 115
EVENINGS OUT 152
examination room
   207
examination table
   207
exchange rate 142
exercise bike 176
exercise book 136
exfoliating
   glove 67
eye 201
eye chart 211
eye drops 211
eyeliner 101
eyeshadow 101
eye test 211
fabric 172
fabric scissors 172

face 202
FAMILY AND FRIENDS 10
farmland 244
fashion 107
FAST FOOD 129
fawn 230
felt-tip pens 136
femur 205
fermented soybean
   paste stew 122
FERRY AND BOAT
   TRAVEL 46
FESTIVALS 252
fever 218
fibula 205
filing cabinet 139
finch 234
finger 201
fingernail 201
fir 242
fire station 146
fireworks 250
first-aid kit 197, 216
First Full Moon Day
   254
fishing 196
FISHMONGER'S 89
five-grain rice and
   nuts 255
fizzy drink 80, 250
flamingo 234
flavoured glutinous
   rice 255
flip-flops 111
flippers 161
floor cushion 127
florist's 115
flowerpot 69
flowerpot stand 69
FLOWERS 240
flute 165
fly 239
flysheet 147
foal 230
folder 139
food and drink 107
food processor 60
foot 202
FOOTBALL 180
football 181
football boots 181
football match 181
football pitch 173, 181
football player 181
footwear 107
forehead 201
forest 244
formula milk 103
foundation 101
fountain 146

fountain pen 136
fox 232
fracture 215
frame 37
frames 211
FRESH AND DAIRY PRODUCTS 96
fridge-freezer 62
fried chicken with spicy sauce 122
frog 236
front door 54
front light 37
FRUIT AND VEGETABLES 83
fruit juice 80
fruit tart 95
frying pan 60
fuel gauge 24
fuel pump 28
Full Moon viewing 256
funfair 154
fungus 242
furniture 107
furniture store 115
fuse box 53
GAMES 168
gaming 149
gangway 47
garage 32, 54
garden centre 115
garden fork 114
gardening gloves 70, 114
gardens 151
garlic 87
gears 37
gear stick 24
gecko 236
GENERAL HEALTH AND WELLBEING 197
giant panda 233
gift 250
gift shop 116
ginger 87
ginseng chicken soup 122
giraffe 233
glacier 244
glass 128
glasses 211
glasses case 211
glove compartment 25
gloves 112
glutinous rice ball doughnuts 124
go 169
goal 173, 181

goalkeeper 181
goat 229
goggles 185
going to karaoke 149
goldfish 228
GOLF 195
golf bag 195
golf ball 195
golf buggy 195
golf club 195
golfer 195
goose 229
go-stop 169
GP 207
grape 85
grapefruit 85
grapevine 242
grasshopper 239
grassland 244
grater 60
graze 215
green 7
green tea 119
greetings card 104, 250
grilled beef 123
grilled fish 123
groundsheet 147
guidebook 151
guinea pig 228
gull 234
gums 209
gutter 54
guy rope 147
gym ball 177
gymnastics 196
gypsophila 241
hair 201
hairbrush 101
hairdresser's 116
hairdryer 67
hairspray 101
ham 93
hammer 113
hammock 161
hamster 229
hand 202
handbag 112
handball 196
handbrake 25
handle 117
handlebars 37
hardware shop 116
hare 232
Harvest Festival 254
head 202
headlight 26
headphones 164
headrest 25

HEALTH 197
heater 54
hedgehog 232
heel 201
helicopter 19
helmet 37, 194
helmet cam 35
herbal medicine 222
heron 234
highchair 103
high heels 112
high jump 192
high-rise block 51
hill 245
hip 203
hippopotamus 233
hob 62
hockey 196
holdall 45
hole punch 136
holiday migration 256
honey 78
honey cookie 124
honeysuckle 242
honey toast 124
horse 229
HOSPITAL 213
hospital 146, 199
hospital bed 213
hot dog 130
HOTEL 155
hotel 146
HOUSE 52
house plant 58
HOUSEWORK 71
humerus 205
hurdles 193
hutch 231
hypnotherapy 222
ice axe 188
ice pack 216
ice skates 188
ice skating 188
ignition 25
ILLNESS 217
in/out tray 139
incubator 220
indicator 26
inflatable dinghy 154
information board 45
INJURY 214
ink 171
INSIDE THE BODY 204
insect repellent 99
instant coffee 78
intercom 56
IN THE HOME 49
IN TOWN 145
iris 241

iron 72
ironing board 72
island 246
ivy 243
jack 32
jacket 110
jam 78, 110
jasmine 241
javelin 193
jaw 201
jeans 110
jellyfish 237
jet ski® 185
jetty 47
jeweller's shop 116
jewellery-making 170
jigsaw puzzle 169
jogging 149
jogging bottoms 110
judo 191
jujitsu 191
jujube 85
jumper 110
jump leads 32
junction 28
kangaroo 233
karaoke 154
kayaking 186
kendo 191
kennel 231
kerb 28
ketchup 78
kettle 60
kettlebell 177
key 56
keyboard 133, 166
key card 157
key fob 56
kickboxing 191
kid 230
killer whale 237
kimchi 123
kimchi stew 123
kingfisher 234
KITCHEN 59
kitchen knife 60
kitchen scales 60
kitchenware 107
kitten 230
kiwi fruit 85
knee 202
kneecap 205
knife and fork 63, 128
knitting needles 172
knot 247
Korean beef 93
KOREAN FESTIVAL CUSTOMS 256
KOREAN FESTIVAL FOOD 255

Korean fish cake 130
Korean flute 166
Korean melon 85
Korean teacup 63
Korean traditional clothing 256
Korean zither 166
KTX 40
labour suite 220
lace-up shoes 112
ladle 60
ladybird 239
lake 245
lamb 230
LAND, SEA, AND SKY 244
lane 28
Lantern Festival 254
laptop 139
lark 234
laundry basket 65
lavender 243
lead 224
leather gloves 35
leather goods 107
leather jacket 35
lecture hall 137
lecturer 137
leg 202
leggings 110
LEISURE 147
leisure centre 175
lemon 85
letter 144
lettuce 87
library 137, 145
lichen 243
lifeboat 48
lifebuoy 47
LIFE EVENTS 251
lifejacket 47, 186
lift 250
lighting 107
light railway 40
lilac 243
lily 241
lily-of-the-valley 241
line judge 183
liner 48
lingerie 107
lion 233
lip balm 101
lipstick 101
listening to music 149
litter tray 231
lizard 236
lobster 91, 237
locomotive 40
long jump 193

lotus root 87
LOUNGE 57
lozenge 99
lucky pouch 247
luggage rack 41
luggage trolley 45
Lunar New Year 254
LUNCH AND DINNER 121
lychee 85
macaroon 95
mackerel 90
magazine 105
magpie 235
maidenhair tree 243
MAMMALS 232
mango 85
map 21, 105
maple 243
marinated crab with soy sauce 123
MARINE CREATURES 237
marsh 245
mascara 101
massage 222
matches 159
mattress 66
mayfly 239
measuring jug 61
medal 175
medicine 199
meditation 222
menu 127
meter 54
metro 41
microwave 62
midwife 220
milk 96
mince 93
minibar 157
MINIBEASTS 238
minibus 34
mirror 66, 68
mittens 102
model-making 170
moist towel 127
mole 232
monitor 213
monkey 233
monkfish 90
monument 151
mooli 87
moon 246
mop 72
mosque 146
mosquito 239
moss 243
moth 239

MOTORBIKE 35
motorbike 35
motorhome 159
motorway 28
mountain 245
mountain bike 194
mouse 133, 232
mouse mat 133
mouth 201
mouth organ 166
mouthwash 100, 209
moxibustion 222
mug 63
mulberry 85
museum 151
MUSIC 163
musical 154
musician 164
music shop 116
mussel 91
muzzle 224
nails 113
nail varnish 101
napkin 64
nappy 103
nappy cream 103
National Liberation Day 254
nausea 218
neck 202
neck brace 213
necklace 112
needle and thread 172
NEWSAGENT AND CONVENIENCE STORE 104
newspaper 105
newt 236
New Year's bow 256
New Year's Eve 254
nightclub 154
noodles 78
noodle soup 121
nose 19, 201
notebook 105
notepad 139
number plate 26
nurse 207
nuts 80
nuts and bolts 113
oak 243
octopus 91
OFFICE 138
office block 146
oil paint 171
ointment 216
olive oil 79
onion 88

opera 154
operating theatre 213
OPTICIAN'S 210
optician's 116, 211
orange 85
orange juice 120
orchestra 164
orchid 241
osteopathy 222
ostrich 235
OTHER SHOPS 115
OTHER SPORTS 196
otter 232
oven 62
owl 235
oxygen mask 213
oyster 91
package 144
paddle 186
paddleboarding 186
paint 113
paintbrush 113, 171
pak choi 88
palace 151
palette 171
palm 201
pancakes 95
pants 110
paper 136
paper bag 76
paper clip 136
papercrafts 170
paper-cutting 171
parasol 162
park 146
parking space 28
parrot 225, 229
party 250
passport 45
pastels 171
patient 199
pavement 28
peach 85
peacock 235
peanut butter 120
pedal 37
pedal bin 61
peeler 61
pelican 235
pelvis 205
pen 105, 136
penalty box 173
pencil 105, 136
pencil case 136
penguin 235
peninsula 246
peony 241
pepper 79
perilla leaves 88

persimmon 85
pestle and mortar 61
pet bowl 231
pet carrier 224
pet food 231
petrol station 28
pet shop 116
pharmacist 199
PHARMACY 97
pharmacy 199
phone case 133
phone shop 116
photocopier 140
PHOTOGRAPHY 167
piano 166
picture 58
pig 229
pigeon 235
piglet 230
pilates 177
pill 99
pillow 66
pilot 45
pine 243
pineapple 86
piste 189
plane 243
PLANET EARTH 225
plant 69
PLANT LIFE 242
plaster 99, 197, 216
plaster cast 213
plastic bag 82
plastic slippers 67
plate 64, 128
platform 41
playground 146
pliers 113
plum 86
podium 175
pole vault 193
police station 146
pollack 90
pomegranate 86
pond 245
popcorn 80
poplar 243
poppy 241
pork cutlet 123
porter 157
porthole 48
postal worker 144
postbox 144
postcard 144
POST OFFICE 143
potato 88
pothole 28
pot stand 64
pottery 171
powder 101

power pack 133
pram 103
prawn 91
PREGNANCY 219
pregnancy test 220
press-ups 177
printer 140
produce 82
protective face mask 99
pruners 114
pump 37
punchbag 191
pupil 136
puppy 230
pushchair 103
pyjamas 110
rabbit 229
RACKET SPORTS 182
radar 48
radiator 54
radius 205
rafting 186
RAIL TRAVEL 38
rainbow 246
Ramadan 254
rash 218
razor 100
reading 149
rearview mirror 25
reception 157
receptionist 157
red 7
red bean bun 95
red bean shaved ice dessert 124
red card 181
red chilli paste 79
red pepper 88
referee 175
reflector 37
reflexology 222
restaurant 154
restaurant car 41
rhinoceros 233
ribs 93, 205
rice 79, 120, 121
rice bowl 64, 128
rice cake 80, 124
rice cake soup 121, 255
rice cake with sweet filling 255
rice porridge 120
rice with vegetables and meat 123
ring binder 140
river 245
road 29
road bike 194

road sign 21
rock pool 246
rocks 245
rolling pin 61
roof 26, 49, 54
rope 188
rose 241
rose of sharon 241
rotor 19
rowing machine 177
rubber gloves 72
rug 58
ruler 136
running 177
running track 193
runny nose 218
runway 45
saddle 37
safe 157
safety deposit box 142
safety pin 172
sailing boat 48
salmon 90
salopettes 189
salt 79
salt and pepper 128
sand 162
sandals 112
sandcastle 161
sandwich 130
sanitary towel 100
sat nav 25
saucepan 61
saucer 117
sausage 93
savoury pancake 123
saw 113
saxophone 166
scales 78
scallop 91
scanner 140
scarf 142
schoolbag 136
scissors 137
scoreboard 175
scourer 72
scratch card 105
screwdriver 113
screws 114
scrub 245
scuba diving 186
SD card 167
sea 162
sea bass 90
sea bream 90
sea cucumber 91
seafood soup 123
seal 237
seashells 161

seasonal vegetables 123
seasoned raw beef 123
seasoned vegetables 255
seatbelt 25
sea urchin 91, 237
seaweed 162
seaweed rice roll 130
security alarm 54
SEEING A DOCTOR 206
serviette 128
sesame oil 79
set meal box 130
sewing machine 172
shampoo 100
shark 237
sharpener 137
shaving foam 100
sheep 229
sheet music 164
sheets 65
shin 202
shirt 110
shoe cupboard 56
shoe shop 116
shooting 196
shopping 149
shopping centre 146
shorts 110
shot put 193
shoulder 203
shower 68
shower cubicle 68
shower gel 100
shower puff 67
showers 175
shrimp 91
shrub 69
shuttlecock 182
side dish 120
sieve 61
SIGHTSEEING 150
sightseeing bus 151
signal box 41
SIM card 133
singer 164
single room 157
sink 62, 68
sit-ups 177
skateboarding 196
sketchpad 172
ski boots 189
ski gloves 189
ski goggles 189
ski helmet 189
ski jacket 189
ski poles 189
skipping rope 177

skirt 110
skis 189
ski suit 189
skull 205
sledge 188
sleeping bag 159
sleepsuit 102
sling 216
slippers 112
slug 239
smartphone 133
smoke alarm 54
smoked duck 93
snail 239
snake 236
sneezing 218
snooker 196
snorkelling 186
snowboard 189
snowboarding boots 189
snow chains 32
snowsuit 102
soap 67, 100
socks 111
sofa 58
soft furnishings 107
soju glass 128
sole 201
sonographer 220
soup 120
soup bowl 64, 128
soybean paste 79
soymilk 96
soy sauce 79
soy sauce and vinegar 128
spade 114
spanner 114
spare wheel 32
sparrow 235
spatula 61
speakers 164
spectators 175
speed camera 29
speedometer 25
spicy rice cakes 130
spicy stir-fried chicken 124
spicy stir-fried octopus 124
spider 239
spikes 193
spinach 88
spine 205
spirits 80
splinter 216
sponge 67
spoon 64, 128
SPORT 173

sports 149
spring onion 88
squash 183
squash ball 183
squash racket 183
squid 91
squirrel 231
stable 231
stadium 175
stairwell 56
stall 82
stamp 105, 144
stands 175
stapler 137
starfish 237
stars 246
starting blocks 193
stationer's 116
steak 93
steamed bun 130
steamed egg 124
steamer 61
steering wheel 25
stepladder 114
stern 48
stethoscope 207
sticky notes 140
sticky tape 140
still water 80
sting 216
stir-fried glass noodles 124
stopwatch 193
stork 235
strawberry 86
stream 245
student 137
studio flat 51
sugar 79
suitcase 45
sun 246
sunburn 216
sun cream 99
sunflower 241
sunglasses 162
sunhat 162
sunset 246
suntan lotion 162
SUPERMARKET 75
surfboard 186
surfing 186
swan 235
sweatshirt 111
sweet pancake 124
sweet potato 88
sweet rice puff 124
sweets 80
swimmer 185
swimming cap 185
swimming pool 185

swimming trunks 162, 185
swimsuit 111, 162, 185
swivel chair 140
syringe 197, 207
table 127
tablecloth 127
table grill 127
tablet 99, 133, 197
table tennis 196
taekwondo 191
tail 19, 225
tampon 100
tangerine 86
tap 62, 68
tape measure 172
tea 120
teabags 79
teacher 137
team 175
teapot 61
tea shop 116
teaspoon 64
tee 195
teeth 209
telephone 140
temple 151
tennis 183
tennis ball 183
tennis court 183
tennis player 183
tennis racket 183
tent 147, 159
tent peg 147
terminal 45
textbook 137
thalassotherapy 222
theatre 154
thermometer 207
thermostat 54
thigh 202
(three-piece) suit 111
thrush 235
thumb 201
tibia 205
ticket 41
ticket barrier 41
ticket machine 29, 41
ticket office 41
tie 111
tiger 233
tights 111
tiles 62, 114
TIME 15
timetable 21
tin opener 61
tissues 59
toad 236
toast 120
toaster 61

toe 201
toenail 201
toilet 68
toilet brush 68
toiletries 157
toilet roll 68
toll point 29
tomato 88
tongs 127
TOOL SHOP 113
toothbrush 100, 209
toothpaste 100, 209
toothpicks 128
torch 159
tornado potato 130
tortoise 236
tour guide 151
tourist office 151
towel 68
towel rail 68
town hall 146
tow truck 32
toys 107
track 41
trader 82
traditional black ink 172
traditional decoration 247
traditional ink painting 171
traditional performance 154

traffic cone 29
traffic lights 29
traffic warden 29
train 41
trainers 112
train station 41
TRANSPORT 19
travel agent's 116
travelling 149
trawler 48
treadmill 177
trellis 70
triangle gimbap 130
tripod 167
trolley 78
trombone 166
trophy 175
trough 231
trousers 111
trowel 70, 114
trout 90
trumpet 166
T-shirt 111
tuba 166
tulip 241
tumble drier 72
tumbler 64
tuna 90
tunnel 29
turtle 236
TV 58
TV stand 58
tweezers 216

twin room 157
tyre 26, 37
ulna 205
ultrasound 220
umbrella 7
umpire 183
umpire's chair 183
USB stick 140
vacuum cleaner 72
valley 245
vegetable oil 73, 79
velodrome 194
Venetian blind 58
vertebrae 205
vest 102
VET 223
vet 224
villa 51
vinegar 79
violin 166
volcano 245
volleyball 196
vulture 235
waffle 95
waiter 127
waiting room 207
waitress 127
walking 149
wallpaper 114
walnut ball cake 124
ward 213
wardrobe 66
warning triangle 32

washing line 72
washing machine 72
washing powder 72
wasp 239
wastepaper basket 72
watching TV/films 149
water bottle 194
watercolours 172
water cooler 62
watering can 70, 114
watermelon 86
water polo 185
waterproof jacket 111
waterskiing 186
WATER SPORTS 184
waves 162
WEATHER 18
weedkiller 70
weightlifting 177
weightlifting bench 177
WELLBEING 176
wetsuit 186
wet wipes 103
whale 237
wheel 26, 37
wheelchair 213
whisk 62
whistle 181
white 7
whiteboard 137

wholemeal bread 95
willow 243
window 26, 49, 54
window box 70
windscreen 26
windscreen wiper 26
windsurfing 186
wine 80
wine glass 64
wing 26
wing mirror 26
WINTER SPORTS 187
wireless router 133
wolf 232
wooden floor 58
wooden spoon 62
woodlouse 239
woodwork 171
woolly hat 112
WORK 13
worktop 62
wrench 114
wrist 201
X-ray 213
xylophone 166
yacht 48
yellow 7
yellow card 181
yoga 177
yoghurt 96, 120
yunnori 169
zebra crossing 29
Zimmer frame® 213

가구 107
가구점 115
가리비 91
가사 71
가수 164
가슴 202
가시 박힘 216
가야금 166
가위 137
가정용 직물 제품 107
가족과 친구 10
가죽 제품 107
가죽장갑 35
가죽점퍼 35
가지 86
가축과 조류 227
간장 79
간장게장 123
간장과 식초 128
간호사 207
갈매기 234
갈비 93
갈비찜 122
갈퀴 114
감 85
감자 88
감자칩 80
감자칼 61
갑판 48
갑판 의자 161
강 245
강사 137
강아지 230
강의실 137
강정 124
강판 60
개 228
개구리 236
개미 238
개울 245
개집 231

개찰구 41
객차 40
거미 239
거북 236
거실 57
거울 66, 68
거위 229
거즈 216
거품기 62
건강 176
건강 207
걷기 149
걸레 71
검도 191
검은색 7
게 91, 237
게임 149
겨울 스포츠 187
겨울우주복 102
격자울타리 70
격투 스포츠 190
견과류 80
견인차 32
경골 205
경기장 175
경륜장 194
경전철 40
경주용 트랙 193
경찰서 146
계기판 24
계단실 56
계란 91
계란찜 124
계량기 54
계량컵 61
계산서 127
고구마 88
고등어 90
고래 237
고무 보트 48
고무장갑 72

고속 도로 28
고속열차 40
고스톱 169
고슴도치 232
고양이 228
고양이 배변판 231
고추 87
고추장 79
고층아파트 51
골 173, 181
골기퍼 181
골동품 가게 115
골반 205
골절상 215
골짜기 245
골프 195
골프 가방 195
골프 공 195
골프 선수 195
골프 채 195
골프 카트 195
곰 233
공공 체육 시설 175
공구가게 113
공기 펌프 37
공원 146
공작새 235
공책 105
공항 44
곶감 124
과일 타르트 95
과일과 야채 83
과일주스 80
과자 78
과자류 104
관광 150
관광 안내서 151
관광 안내소 151
관광 안내원 151
관광 지도 151
관광버스 151

관목 69
관목 덤불 245
관중 175
관중석 175
관현악단 164
광복절 254
교과서 137
교실 135
교육 134
교정 137
교통 19
교회 145
구강 세정제 100, 209
구급 상자 197, 216
구덩이 28
구명보트 48
구명조끼 47, 186
구명튜브 47
구역질 218
국 120
국그릇 64, 128
국수 121
국자 60
국화 240
굴 91
굴뚝 54
궁 151
권투 글러브 191
권투 링 191
귀 201
귀걸이 112
귀뚜라미 238
균류 242
귤 86
그림 58
극장 154
글로브박스 25
금고 157
금붕어 228
금은방 116
기관차 40

기내 45
기념비 151
기니피그 228
기린 233
기본 어휘 및 표현 8,
20, 50, 74, 118, 148, 174,
198, 226, 248
기수 19
기어 37
기저귀 103
기저귀 가방 102
기저귀 크림 103
기차 41
기차역 38
기차역 41
기침 218
기침약 99
기타 종목 196
길거리 공연 153
김밥 130
김치 123
김치찌개 123
깁스 213
까마귀 234
까치 235
깻잎 88
꼬리빗 101
꽃 240
꽃 가게 115
꽃다발 250
꿀 78
끈 달린 신발 112
나무 주걱 62
나물 123, 255
나방 239
나비 238
나사 113
나이트클럽 154
나이프와 포크 63, 128
낙타 233
낚시 196
낚지볶음 124
난방기 54

난초 241
날씨 18
남성용 수영복 162, 185
내비게이션 25
냄비 60
냄비받침 64
냅킨 64, 128
냉면 122
냉장고 62
너트와 볼트 113
넥타이 111
노 186
노란색 7
노래방 154
노래방 가기 149
노리개 장식 247
노점 82
노트북 139
녹나무 242
녹차 119
놀이 168
놀이터 146
농구 179
농구 선수 179
농구 시합 179
농구 코트 179
농구공 179
농구화 179
농산품 82
농어 90
농지 244
높이뛰기 192
누전 차단기 53
눈 201
늑골 205
늑대 232
다람쥐 232
다른 상점 115
다리 28, 202
다리미 72
다리미판 72
다이빙대 185
다진 고기 93

다트 169
단것 80
단독주택 51
단소 166
단오제 254
단추 172
단팥빵 95
단풍나무 243
달 246
달리기 177
달맞이 256
달팽이 239
닭 229
닭갈비 123
담배 104
담쟁이덩굴 243
당근 86
당김줄 147
당나귀 229
당신에 대하여 9
닻 47
대걸레 72
대구 90
대기실 207
대나무 242
대여 금고 142
대왕판다 233
대체의학 221
대추 85
대퇴골 205
대형 버스 34
더블 룸 157
더블 베이스 165
데이지 240
도넛 95
도로 29
도롱뇽 236
도마 60
도마뱀 236
도마뱀붙이 236
도미 90
도서관 137, 146
도시락 130

도어매트 56
도예 171
독서 149
독수리 235
돈가스 123
돌고래 237
동굴 244
동물병원 223
동전 76
돛단배 48
돼지 229
된장 79
된장찌개 122
두개골 205
두꺼비 236
두더지 232
두루미 234
두유 96
뒤꿈치 201
뒤집개 61
드라이기 67
드라이버 113
드럼 165
드론 167
득점 게시판 175
등 203
디에스엘아르 167
딱정벌레 238
딸기 86
땀 억제제 100
땅, 바다, 그리고 하늘
244
땅콩버터 120
때수건 67
떡 80, 124
떡국 121, 255
떡볶이 130
뜨개바늘 172
뜸 요법 222
라디에이터 54
라마단 254
라벤더 243
라일락 243

라켓 스포츠 182
래프팅 186
랩 59
러그 58
러닝머신 177
레깅스 110
레드 카드 181
레몬 85
레이더 48
렌치 114
로드 바이크 194
로잉 머신 177
로터헤드 19
롤빵 95
리드줄 224
리치 85
린스 100
립밤 101
립스틱 101
링거 주사 213
마늘 87
마룻바닥 58
마스카라 101
마스크 99
마우스 133
마우스 패드 133
마카롱 95
만년필 136
만담 154
만두 122
만화책 104
말 229
말똥가리 234
말벌 239
망고 85
망아지 230
망치 113
매니큐어 101
매듭술 247
매트리스 247
매표소 41
맥주 80
맥주잔 127

머그잔 63
머리 202
머리 받침대 25
머리카락 201
먹물 80
멀리뛰기 193
메뉴판 127
메달 175
메뚜기 239
멜론 84
멜빵 바지 110
멧돼지 232
면 78
면도칼 100
면봉 103
면세점 45
멸치 90
명상 222
명절 대이동 256
명절 음식 255
명절 풍속 256
명절과 축제 247
명태 90
모기 239
모니터 213
모래 162
모래성 161
모스크 146
모종삽 70, 114
목 202
목 보호대 213
목걸이 112
목공예 171
목발 213
목캔디 99
몸속 204
못 113
무 87
무궁화 241
무당벌레 239
무릎 202
무선 공유기 133
무지개 246

문 26
문구점 116
문어 91
물 80
물뿌리개 70, 114
물수건 127
물안경 185
물약 99
물잔 64
물집 215
물총새 234
물통 194
물티슈 103
뮤지컬 154
미니바 157
미루나무 243
미술과 공예 170
미술관 151
미용실 116
민달팽이 239
민들레 240
밀대 61
밀크커피 117, 119
바 127, 153
바게트 95
바구니 73, 78
바나나 73, 84
바늘과 실 172
바다 162
바다거북 236
바다표범 237
바닷가재 91, 237
바둑 169
바디슈트 102
바스켓 179
바위 245
바이올린 166
바지 111
바퀴 26, 37
바퀴벌레 238
박물관 151
박쥐 232
반도 246

반려견 방석 231
반바지 110
반사 요법 222
반찬 120
반창고 99, 197, 216
발 202
발가락 201
발레 153
발목 201
발바닥 201
발진 218
발톱 201
밤나무 242
밥 120, 121
밥그릇 64, 128
방갈로 51
방석 127
방수 재킷 111
방수깔개 147
방수천 147
방충제 99
"방해하지 마시오"
　　표시 157
방향지시등 26
배 202
배구 196
배드민턴 182
배드민턴 채 182
배수관 54
배추 87
배트 178
백미러 25
백조 235
백합 241
백화점 106
백화점 115
뱀 236
버거 130
버너 195
버드나무 243
버섯 87
버스 33
버스 34

버즘나무 243
버터 96
번호판 26
벌 238
벌레 238
벌쏘임 216
범고래 237
범퍼 26
법원 145
벙어리장갑 102
벚꽃 축제 253
벚꽃나무 242
베개 66
베란다 69
베란다 49
베이스 기타 165
베이스 드럼 165
베이컨 93
벨 37
벨트 111
벽지 114
변기 68
변기솔 68
변속 레버 24
별 246
병실 213
병원 212
병원 146, 199
병원 방문 206
병원 침대 213
보닛 26
보드게임 169
보디보딩 185
보쌈 122
보안경보기 54
보일러 53
보조 배터리 팩 133
보행 보조기 213
복도 157
복사기 140
복숭아 85
복주머니 247
볼 201

볼 걸 183
볼 보이 183
볼링 169
볼펜 136
봉투 104, 144
부동산 중개소 115
부동산 32
부상 214
부스터 케이블 32
부엉이 235
부엌칼 60
부츠 35
부침개 123
부표 47
부항 요법 221
분기점 28
분만실 220
분말 세제 72
분수 146
분유 103
불가사리 237
불고기 123
불꽃놀이 250
불판 127
붓 171
붕대 98, 197, 216
뷰티 살롱 115
브레이크 37
브로콜리 86
블라우스 109
블라인드 58
블러셔 101
블루베리 84
비누 67, 100
비닐봉투 82
비둘기 235
비빔밥 123
비엠엑스 194
비치 볼 161
비키니 109
비키니 수영복 161
비행기 여행 42
빗 101

빗자루 71
빙하 244
빨간색 7
빨래 건조대 71
빨래건조기 72
빨래바구니 65
빨래집게 72
빨랫줄 72
빵 73
빵집과 제과점 94
뽁뽁이 144
사격 196
사과 84
사다새 235
사랑앵무 228
사막 244
사무실 138
사무실 건물 146
사슴 232
사육장 231
사이드 미러 26
사이클 194
사인펜 136
사자 233
사진 58
사진기 151
사진기 렌즈 167
사진촬영 167
산 245
산림 244
산소 마스크 213
산악 자전거 194
산토끼 232
산호 237
산호초 246
살구 84
삼각김밥 130
삼각대 167
삼겹살 122
삼계탕 122
삽 114
상어 237
상완골 205

상인 82
상자 82, 144
상점 73
새끼 고양이 230
새끼 돼지 230
새끼 사슴 230
새끼 양 230
새끼 염소 230
새우 91
새장 70, 231
색소폰 166
색연필 135
샌드백 191
샌드위치 130
샌들 112
생강 87
생리대 100
생선가게 89
생선구이 123
생쥐 232
샤워 젤 100
샤워기 68
샤워볼 67
샤워실 68
샤워장 175
샴푸 100
서랍 62
서랍장 66
서류장 139
서류철 140
서류함 139
서예 170
서예붓 171
서점 115
서프보드 186
서핑 186
석가 탄신일 253
석류 86
선글라스 162
선두 48
선로 41
선물 250
선물 가게 116

선미 48
선반 41
선생님 137
선심판 183
선창 47
선크림 99
설날 254
설탕 79
섬 246
성게 91, 237
성냥 159
성묘 256
성탄절 254
세면대 68
세면도구 157
세배 256
세차장 28
세탁기 72
세탁소 145
센터 서클 173
셀러리 87
셔츠 110
셔틀콕 182
소고기 버거 93
소금 79
소금과 후추 128
소나무 243
소독용 크림 98
소방서 146
소스냄비 61
소시지 93
소주잔 128
소쿠리 60
소파 58
소포 144
소형 버스 34
속도 감시 카메라 29
속도계 25
손 202
손가락 201
손님 82
손목 201
손바닥 201

손잡이 56, 117
손전등 159
손톱 201
솜 103
송아지 230
송어 90
송편 255
쇄골 205
쇼핑 149
쇼핑몰 146
쇼핑카트 78
수건 68
수건걸이 68
수구 185
수납장 68
수달 232
수도꼭지 62, 68
수리 234
수목화 171
수박 86
수상 스키 타기 186
수상 스포츠 184
수선화 240
수세미 72
수술실 213
수영 선수 185
수영모 185
수영장 185
수의사 224
수족관 231
수채화 물감 172
수첩 139
수하물 찾는 곳 44
수하물 카트 45
순대 130
숟가락 64, 128
쉐이빙폼 100
슈퍼마켓 77
스노보드 189
스노보드 화 189
스노체인 32
스노클링 186
스누커 196

(스리피스) 정장 111
스마트폰 133
스웨터 110
스카치테이프 140
스카프 112
스캐너 140
스케이트 188
스케이트 타기 188
스케이트보드 타기 196
스케치북 172
스쿠버 다이빙 186
스쿼시 183
스쿼시 공 183
스쿼시 채 183
스키 189
스키 고글 189
스키 장갑 189
스키 재킷 189
스키 헬멧 189
스키바지 189
스키폴 189
스키화 189
스타킹 111
스타팅 블록 193
스테이크 93
스톱워치 193
스파이크 슈즈 193
스패너 114
스페어타이어 32
스펀지 67
스피커 164
슬개골 205
슬리퍼 112, 161
습지 245
승강장 41
승마 196
시간 15
시간표 21
시금치 88
시내 145
시동장치 25
시력 검사 211
시력 검사표 211

시리얼 119
시상대 175
시장 81
시청 146
시트 튜브 37
식기 건조대 62
식당 154
식당칸 41
식물 242
식사공간 63
식용유 73, 79
식음료 107
식초 79
신문 105
신문 가판대와 편의점 104
신발 107
신발 가게 116
신발장 56
신선 제품과 유제품 96
신용 카드 76, 142
신체 200
신호등 29
신호소 41
실내 자전거 176
실내용 가운 110
실내용 화초 58
실로폰 166
심 카드 133
심벌즈 165
심판 175, 183
심판석 183
십자말풀이 169
십자수 170
싱글 룸 157
싱크대 62
쌀 79
썰매 188
쓰레기봉투 71, 76
쓰레받기 72
아귀 90
아기 욕조 103
아기 의자 103

아기 침대 103
아기신발 102
아기용품 102
아기우주복 102
아령 176
아스파라거스 86
아이라이너 101
아이리스 241
아이섀도 101
아이스박스 159
아이젠 188
아침식사 119
아코디언 165
아파트 49
악기점 116
악보 164
악어 236
안개꽃 241
안경 211
안경점 210
안경店 116, 211
안경집 211
안경테 211
안내판 45
안마 222
안장 37
안전 삼각대 32
안전벨트 25
안테나 54
알람 시계 65
알약 99, 197
암벽 등반 196
암소 229
앞유리 26
애벌레 238
애완 동물 용품점 116
애완동물 넥카라 224
애완동물 목걸이 224
애완동물 사료 231
애완동물 식기 231
액세서리 107
앵무새 229
야구 178

야구 경기 178
야구 글러브 178
야구 모자 111, 178
야구 선수 178
야구공 178
약 199
약과 124
약국 97
약국 199
약사 199
약식 255
양 229
양궁 196
양귀비 241
양념치킨 122
양동이 71
양동이와 삽 161
양말 111
양배추 86
양상추 87
양서류와 파충류 236
양파 88
어깨 203
어린이날 253
어묵 130
언덕 245
얼굴 202
얼음 도끼 188
얼음주머니 216
엄지발가락 201
엄지손가락 201
엉덩이 203
에센셜 오일 222
에스디 카드 167
에어 매트 159
에어백 32
에클레어 95
엑스레이 213
엘리베이터 56
여가활동 147
여권 45
여물통 231
여성 속옷 107

여성용 구두 112
여우 232
여행 149
여행 가방 45
여행사 116
연고 216
연근 87
연락선과 배 여행 46
연료계 24
연못 245
연석 28
연습장 136
연어 90
연필 105, 136
연필깎이 137
열 218
열쇠 56
열쇠고리 56
염소 229
엽서 105, 144
영화관 145, 154
영화 보기 149
옐로 카드 181
오곡밥과 견과류 255
오디 85
오렌지 85
오렌지 주스 120
오로라 246
오리 229
오리발 161
오븐 62
오소리 232
오이 87
오징어 91
오토바이 35
오토바이 35
오페라 154
온도 조절기 54
올리브 오일 79
옷걸이 65
옷장 66
옷핀 172
와이퍼 26

와인 80
와인잔 64
와플 95
왜가리 234
외식 125
외양간 231
외투 109
요가 177
요골 205
요구르트 96, 120
요리 149
요트 48
욕실 67
욕조 68
우리 231
우산 7
우승컵 175
우유 96
우체국 143
우체국 직원 144
우체통 144
우표 105, 144
운동 173
운동 149
운동복 상의 111
운동화 112
운전 27
운하선 48
원룸 51
원반던지기 192
원뿔 표지판 29
원숭이 233
원예용 가위 114
원예용 장갑 70, 114
원피스 수영복 111, 162, 185
원피스 스키복 189
웨이트 트레이닝 177
웨이트 트레이닝 기구 177
웨트슈트 186
윈드서핑 186
윗몸 일으키기 177

유도 191
유등 축제 254
유모차 103
유아식 102
유에스비 스틱 140
유화 물감 141
육상 경기 192
육상 선수 192
육식 동물 새끼 230
육회 123
윷놀이 169
은방울꽃 241
은행 141
은행나무 243
음악 163
음악 듣기 149
음악가 164
의류 107
의류와 신발 108
의사 199
의자 127
이끼 243
이동 유원지 154
이동장 224
이마 201
이발소 115
이불 66
이쑤시개 128
이어폰 164
이젤 171
인도 28
인동 242
인사 카드 104, 250
인생에서 겪는 큰 일 251
인쇄기 140
인스턴트 커피 78
인큐베이터 220
인터폰 56
일, 월, 그리고 계절 16
일광 화상 216
일몰 246

일반 건강과 웰빙 12
일반의사 207
일상생활 7, 17
임신 219
임신 테스트 220
입 201
입구 55
입구 54
입마개 224
잇몸 209
잉어 90
잉크 171
자 136
자동차 22
자동차 전시장 115
자두 86
자몽 85
자수 170
자전거 36
자전거 자물쇠 37
작약 241
잔 117, 128
잔 받침 117
잠옷 110
잠자리 238
잡지 105
잡채 124
장갑 112
장구 166
장기 169
장난감 107
장대높이뛰기 193
장미 241
장식장 57
장식품 250
장신구 세공 170
장애물 달리기 193
장어 90, 237
재단 가위 172
재봉틀 172
재스민 241
재채기 218
재킷 110

잭 32
잼 78, 119
저녁 외출 152
저울 78
저택 51
전기 기타 165
전기밥솥 60
전나무 242
전복 91
전자 제품 가게 115
전자레인지 62
전조등 26, 37
전통 공연 154
전화기 140
절 151
절굿공이와 절구 61
절벽 246
절상 215
점심식사와 저녁식사 121
점안액 211
접시 64, 128
접이식 사다리 114
접착 테이프 216
젓가락 64, 128
정강이 202
정골 요법 222
정기선 48
정비소 32
정수기 62
정원 151
정월 대보름 254
정육점 92
젖병 102
제야 254
제조제 70
제트 스키 185
조개 91
조개껍질 161
조깅 149
조류 234
조리대 62
조립마루 69

조명 107
조산사 220
조수 웅덩이 246
조종사 45
조종석 19, 45
종달새 234
종아리 203
종아리뼈 205
종업원 127
종이 136
종이 자르기 171
종이공예 170
종이봉투 76
주거생활 49
주방 59
주방용 저울 60
주방용품 107
주사기 197, 207
주사위 169
주유기 28
주유소 28
주전자 60
주짓수 191
주차 공간 28
주차 단속원 29
주차장 28
주키니호박 87
주택 52
죽 120
죽순 86
줄 188
줄넘기 줄 177
줄자 172
중정형주택 51
쥐며느리 239
즉석복권 105
증류주 80
지구 225
지네 238
지도 21, 105
지렁이 239
지붕 26, 49, 54
지빠귀 235

지우개 135
지의류 243
지폐 76, 142
지하철 41
지휘자 164
직불 카드 76, 142
직업 13
직접 수리·조립하기
   149
진공청소기 72
진료실 207
진찰대 207
질병 217
짐 볼 177
집게 127
찌르레기 234
찜기 61
찜닭 122
차 120
차 파는 가게 116
차고 54
차량 고장 30
차례 256
차례 음식 255
차선 28
찬장 62
찰과상 215
참기름 79
참나무 243
참새 235
참외 85
참치 90
찹쌀도넛 124
찻잔 63
찻주전자 61
창문 26, 49, 54
창틀화분 70
책 104
책가방 136
책상 139
책장 57
챙 넓은 모자 162
척골 205

척추 205
척추 지압법 221
척추골 205
천 172
천장 선풍기 53
철물점 116
청경채 88
청바지 110
청진기 207
체 61
체리 84
체스 169
체온계 207
체인 37
체조 196
첼로 165
초록색 7
초원 244
초음파 220
초음파 검사자 220
초인종 56
초코잼 119
초콜릿 80
초콜릿 박스 250
최면 요법 222
추석 254
축구 180
축구 경기 181
축구 경기장 181
축구 선수 181
축구공 181
축구장 173
축구화 181
축제 252
출발 안내 전광판 40
충전기 132
치과 208
치과 간호사 209
치과 의사 209
치과 의자 209
치과 천공기 209
치마 110
치실 209

치아 209
치아 교정기 209
치약 100, 209
침구 65
침낭 159
침대 66
침대 객실 40
침대시트 65
침대조명 66
침술 221
침실 65
침팬지 233
칫솔 100, 209
카나리아 228
카네이션 240
카누 타기 185
카드 169
카드 단말기 76
카드식 열쇠 157
카약 타기 186
카지노 154
카페 145
칼라 201
캔버스 171
캠핑 158
캠핑 트레일러 159
캠핑카 159
캡슐 98
캥거루 233
커튼 57, 66
커피 130
컴팩트 카메라 167
컴퓨터 132
컵라면 130
케이블 132
케이크 250
케첩 79
케틀 벨 177
코 201
코끼리 233
코뿔소 233
콘돔 99
콘서트 154

콘택트 렌즈 211
콘택트 렌즈 보관
   용기 211
콘퍼런스 센터 145
콜리플라워 87
콧물 218
콩새 234
쿠션 58
크로스 트레이너 176
크루아상 95
크림 96
큰 손가방 45
클라리넷 165
클립 136
키보드 133, 166
키위 61
키친타월 59
킥복싱 191
타박상 215
타이어 26, 37
타일 62, 114
타조 235
탁구 196
탄산음료 80, 250
탈의실 175
탐폰 100
탑 튜브 37
탑승 수속 창구 45
탑승권 44
태권도 191
태닝 로션 162
태블릿 피시 133
터널 29
터미널 45
턱 201
턱끝 201
턱받이 102
털모자 112
털실 뭉치 172
테니스 183
테니스 공 183
테니스 선수 183
테니스 채 183

테니스장 183
테이블 127
테이블로 127
텐트 147, 159
텐트 말뚝 147
토끼 229
토마토 88
토스터 61
토스트 120
톨게이트 29
톱 113
통기타 165
통밀빵 95

통신수단과 정보기술
131

통조림 따개 61
투망어선 48
투창 193
투포환 193
튜바 166
튤립 241
트랩 47
트럼펫 166
트렁크 26
트레이닝 바지 110
트롬본 166
트윈 룸 157
틀니 209
티 195
티백 79
티브이 58
티브이 장식장 58
티브이 보기 149
티셔츠 111
티스푼 64
팀 175
파 88
파도 162
파라솔 162
파란색 7
파리 239
파스텔 171
파우더 101

파운데이션 101
파이 95
파인애플 86
파일 139
파티 250
파프리카 88
팔 202
팔 굽혀 펴기 177
팔 튜브 185
팔걸이 붕대 216
팔꿈치 203
팔레트 171
팔찌 111
팝콘 80
팥빙수 124
패들보드 타기 186
패스트푸드 129
팬케이크 95
팬티 110
퍼즐 맞추기 169
펀치 136
페널티 박스 173
페달 37
페달 휴지통 61
페인트 113
페인트 붓 113
펜 105
펜더 26
펜치 113
펭귄 235
편백나무 242
편의점 115
편지 144
포대기 103
포도 85
포도 덩굴 242
포스트잇 140
포유류 232
포일 59
포터 157
폭포 245
폰 케이스 133
표 41

표 판매기 29, 41
표지판 21
푸드 프로세서 60
프라모델 조립 170
프라이팬 60
프런트 157
플라스틱 슬리퍼 67
플루트 165
피아노 166
핀셋 216
필라테스 177
필통 136
하루살이 239
하마 233
하모니카 166
하얀색 7
하이힐 196
하키 196
하프 165
학생 136, 137
학생 식당 137
한복 256
한약 222
한우 93
합기도 191
합창단 164
핫도그 130
항공기 44
해 246
해먹 246
해물탕 123
해바라기 241
해변 160
해변용 수건 162
해삼 91
해수 요법 222
해안 246
해양생물 237
해초 162
해파리 237
핸드 브레이크 25
핸드백 112
핸드볼 196

핸드폰 가게 116
핸들 25, 37
햄 93
햄스터 7
허니브레드 124
허리 203
허벅지 202
헛간 231
헤드폰 164
헤어스프레이 101
헬리콥터 19
헬멧 35, 37, 194
헬멧에 다는 카메라 35
현관문 54
현금 자동 입출금기
142
현장 48
혈압계 207
협탁 66
호두과자 124
호떡 124
호랑이 233
호루라기 181
호빵 130
호수 245
호치키스 137
호텔 155
호텔 146
호텔 직원 157
홈통 54
홍학 234
홍합 91
화구 62
화분 69
화분 진열대 69
화산 245
화상 215
화원 115
화이트보드 137
화장대 65
화장지 68
화장품 107
화장품 가게 100

화재경보기 54
화초 69
환율 142
환자 199
환전소 142
활강코스 189

활주로 45
황새 235
회오리 감자 130
회전 날개 19
회전의자 140
횡단보도 29

후드 60
후미 19
후미등 37
후추 79
훈제오리 93
휠체어 213

휴지통 72
흉골 205
흰 비둘기 234

PHOTO CREDITS

Shutterstock: p21 timetable (Brendan Howard), p26 red car (JazzBoo), p29 ticket machine (Balakate), p34 minibus (Iakov Filimonov), p40 KTX (Travelerpix), p40 light railway (Bikeworldtravel), p40 departure board (Ki young), p40 locomotive (NGCHIYUI), p41 platform (Phuong D. Nguyen), p41 ticket machine (Balakate), p41 ticket office (Ng KW), p41 train (NGCHIYUI), p41 train station (T.Dallas), p82 marketplace (wizdata), p104 confectionery (Bitkiz), p107 cosmetics (mandritoiu), p107 food and drink (1000 words), p107 footwear (Toshio Chan), p107 kitchenware (NikomMaelao Production), p107 toys (Zety Akhzar), p115 electrical retailer (BestPhotoPlus), p115 estate agency (Barry Barnes), p116 gift shop (Pamela Loreto Perez), p116 pet shop (BestPhotoPlus), p116 tea shop (Zvonimir Atletic), p137 campus (EQRoy), p142 bureau de change (Lloyd Carr), p144 postbox (Johnathan21), p144 stamp (Irisphoto1), p145 church (Ilya Images), p145 conference centre (lou armor), p145 courthouse (Jisoo Song), p146 fire station (KIM JIHYUN), p146 police station (Chintung Lee), p146 shopping centre (rullala), p146 town hall (Subodh Agnihotri), p151 monument (Claudine Van Massenhove), p151 palace (Benz Photograph), p151 sightseeing bus (Roman Sigaev), p151 temple (Mali lucky), p153 busking (iamtui7), p154 casino (Benny Marty), p154 crosstalk (windmoon), p154 musical (Igor Bulgarin), p154 opera (criben), p154 traditional performance (Jack.Q), p164 choir (Marco Saroldi), p164 orchestra (Ferenc Szelepcsenyi), p179 basketball shoes (Milos Vucicevic), p180 football pitch (Christian Bertrand), p183 line judge (Leonard Zhukovsky), p183 umpire (Stuart Slavicky), p186 rafting (novak.elcic), p194 velodrome (Pavel L Photo and Video), p196 handball (Dziurek), p196 table tennis (Stefan Holm), p220 labour suite (ChameleonsEye), p253 Cherry Blossom Festival (Guitar photographer), p253 Children's Day (Igor Bulgarin), p254 Danoje Festival (Kobby Dagan), p254 Lantern Festival (Kobby Dagan), p254 National Liberation Day (Stock for you), p255 ancestral rites food (BYUNGSUK KO), p256 ancestral grave visit (Yeongsik Im), p256 ancestral rites (BYUNGSUK KO), p256 holiday migration (ianden). All other images from Shutterstock.